Surprise package

When God wrecks our plans

Steve Crowter

DayOne

© Day One Publications 2003
First printed 2003

Scripture quotations are from The New International Version unless otherwise stated.
© 1973, 1978, 1984, International Bible Society. Published by Hodder and Stoughton.

British Library Cataloguing in Publication Data available

ISBN 1 903087 38 -4

9 781903 087381

Published by Day One Publications
3 Epsom Business Park, Kiln Lane, Epsom, Surrey KT17 1JF.
☎ 01372 728 300 FAX 01372 722 400
email—sales@dayone.co.uk
www.dayone.co.uk

Designed by Steve Devane and printed by CPD

Dedication

To the memory of Heidi's grandfathers,
David Crowter and John Burch, who loved
her as she loved them

Acknowledgements

My thanks to all who have helped in the production of this book, especially my brother Phil and sister Rosie for their merciless criticism and helpful advice. I would like to express my gratitude to my wife Liz, for her unfailing encouragement and enthusiasm; and the many hours spent reliving often painful memories. I have written the book, but the sections headed with Liz's photograph are very much from her perspective.

Above all, Liz and I thank God for so many things which will become apparent as you read on. We hope and pray that you will find this book helpful and enjoyable.

Contents

Foreword

DAN

Heidi is funny, cute and generous. She is often laughing and if a problem comes she never gets mad, she just says "Oh well", and if she makes a mistake she says "Oops," or laughs like a maniac.

She likes to play sport, especially cricket. We laugh with her because if any of us hits the ball (including her) she shouts "OUT!".

I wish my Mum and Dad would adopt children with Downs, especially if the were like Heidi, but then they'd always be suffering from stress.

Enjoy the book!

From Dan!

HEIDI

I hope you enjoy my book.

love Heidi

Steve Crowter

In she bounced, face split with a huge irresistible grin, laughing blue eyes full of the joy of being alive. She pushed the stray wisps of long blonde hair from her face. 'Hello my mummy darlin'. Hello my daddy sir. I been to school. I been a good girl for Mrs Hemming and Miss Fenlon.'

Her podgy starfish hands poked out of bright red sleeves. They were rolled up of course, because you can't get uniforms for reception children the size of two-year-olds. Still, at least the overlong skirt covered most of her legs. The veins stood out purple if they got too cold, making her look like a piece of corned beef. And of course we could always see the secret hidden beneath the proudly worn school emblem on her jumper; that angry white vertical line dividing her chest.

'Hello Heidi', we smiled back fondly at our beautiful little girl. Just a simple everyday scene, but one far beyond our wildest imaginings those five short years ago.

Liz Crowter

'Nothing can happen to us this year that is unknown to God. He knows all the way ahead that he has planned for us.'

As I sat in church listening to Pastor Paul's New Year sermon my hand wandered down to the newly burgeoning bump beneath my dress. Inwardly I smiled contentedly. It promised to be an exciting year, with the birth of our third child to look forward to. Hopefully a girl, but I would be happy with either as long as everything was all right…

'If, as a Christian, you are anxious about the future, you are not trusting God as you should.

'Never a burden he cannot bear, never a friend like Jesus'.

I jerked back to full attention and the words Paul was quoting imprinted themselves on my brain. Later I wrote them out and added the piece of paper to all the others stuck around my kitchen. But I had no idea how much I would need to remember their truth during the year ahead.

Born on the third of July

 That feeling was with me again as we drove. I had a good excuse to be going fast, and a ready retort to any expressions of complaint. It was the third time now, but that feeling was still like no other; a stomach-churning cocktail of excitement, anticipation, anxiety, hope. I knew there would be pain—Liz squeezed my hand extremely hard at times on these occasions—but I was prepared to go through that barrier; it would all be worthwhile. The other times had been some of the most magical moments of my life.

 So here we were in the delivery room. I hoped it wouldn't be much longer; I was beginning to feel quite exhausted. The labour had been hard going. I hadn't been able to read any of the magazine I'd surreptitiously slipped into the bag. The midwife had seemed concerned about some of the readouts from the monitor, which had been worrying for a time. The baby hadn't been as active as the nurses would have liked, but perhaps it was a bit sleepy. The most nerve-racking moment was when the heart rate dropped to zero, but apparently the probe had become dislodged at that point. Anyway, things seemed okay now, it was just about to... Yes! It's here! Then that agonisingly long second... 'Waaaaaaaah.' Isn't that the most wonderful sound in the world? Yes, it's a girl! Great, my first daughter! The miracle of a new life was just as powerful as ever. How could anyone see this and not believe in God? Quick check. Head, arms, legs. Two eyes, two ears, one nose. Ten fingers, ten toes. Yep, all present and correct. Perfect! Wrapped contentedly in her blanket, I held her close as she breathed in her new surroundings. So light, so tiny. Red and shrivelled of course, like all babies are, but I didn't notice that. How could those fingernails be so small? Welcome to the world, Heidi Anne, my daughter.

I was soon on the phone; they hadn't banned mobiles from hospitals then: 'Hello mum...yes, it's a girl...Gertrude Hephzibah...yes I am joking, it's Heidi Anne…yes, we thought so too…erm, about seven pounds…hold on. (How much?) Precisely six pounds seven ounces…yes, everything's fine.'

Male midwife indeed. Ouch. He's very pleasant, but how am I supposed to relax? Ooooh… Why did I want another baby? Aaaah! Hope everything's all right… 'HOLD MY HAND!' *Stop talking to the midwife about cars, will you… Eeeeeek… I never want to go through this again. I must be mad, with the boys so young…hope it's a girl…Dan and Tim are lovely but OWWWWW! It's all right for you, sitting there cool as you like. I wish men had babies. Oouugh. Aaaaaahh. Yes, yes, go on. aaaaahhh!* 'Is it all right? What is it?' I held my longed-for daughter close to me. Yes, it was a million times worth all that pain. The family of my imagination was complete, and my world was perfect. I lifted her to smile into her eyes; and as she gazed back the illusion was shattered irrevocably. 'Hello Heidi, I'm your mummy', I whispered, the sentiment freezing on my lips and a cold panic gripping my soul. *Yes, I am, but you aren't the daughter I wanted, the special friend I'd dreamed of.* I turned towards Steve, his face suffused with happiness, a picture of contentment, and smiled weakly. I couldn't bring myself to speak. Surely I was wrong, I must be wrong. But those telltale signs I'd so deeply feared… No, I must be imagining it. I'd checked automatically because this was the nightmare scenario, the dread outcome I had never been able to banish from the depths of my mind since that dream two weeks before. I must have been more worried than I had thought—that must be making me think she really did have it. I looked again, but her eyes were still the same. The dream was becoming reality. I had to tell him. 'I think she has got Down's syndrome' I blurted.

My brain would not accept what my ears had heard. My heart was suddenly racing, my mind and face numb as I looked again at the little girl lying contentedly on Liz's chest. No, this wasn't happening to me. 'I remember being a bit worried when Tim was born because he looked like that', I replied eventually, 'I think she's all right'. Liz seemed somewhat reassured, but my peace had gone, my mind in turmoil. *She must be all right. Isn't she? She has to be. SHE HAS TO BE.*

The two midwives came back into the room. 'Have you noticed anything about your baby?' the senior asked gently. 'I think she has got Down's syndrome', replied Liz. The midwife nodded sadly, 'We think she might have too, although we could be wrong. We'd like to get the paediatrician to check her over'. Another nail crashed into our family portrait and we waited sombrely for the paediatrician to arrive.

'I hear this baby has some problems'. Her matter-of-fact tones stabbed my sensitised emotions. *She didn't say 'this baby **may** have some problems'.* My slippery fingerhold on the flotsam of hope loosened a little further. She spoke as she checked eyes and nose, hands and toes. 'Do you know what Down's syndrome means?' 'Yes', replied Liz. Her cousin had Down's. She had died at the age of three. Liz had also worked with children and adults with Down's on a college placement. 'We'll do a blood test to be absolutely sure', the doctor said as she placed her stethoscope on Heidi's chest, 'but she has all the signs. They often have heart problems, but this one seems fine. I can't hear any murmurs.' Then she was off, leaving us to pick out the shards of our exploded world.

The following hours were a step removed from reality, as if I were an actor in someone else's tragedy. There were more phone calls of course, the hardest I'd ever had to make. The last thing I wanted to do was watch the child being bathed, but Liz thought we should. I suppose she was trying to take a first tentative step towards acceptance. As the nurse washed the floppy body I stood in silence and felt nothing.

 Pastor Paul came to visit us that evening. He cradled Heidi in his arms and seemed to have such love for her. I was filled with guilt; I was her mother and didn't feel I loved her at all. She wasn't the normal little girl I would have loved so much, she was something quite different. Paul reminded us of the verse from which he had preached the previous evening: '**Nothing can separate us from the love of God.**' I believed this in my head, but my heart

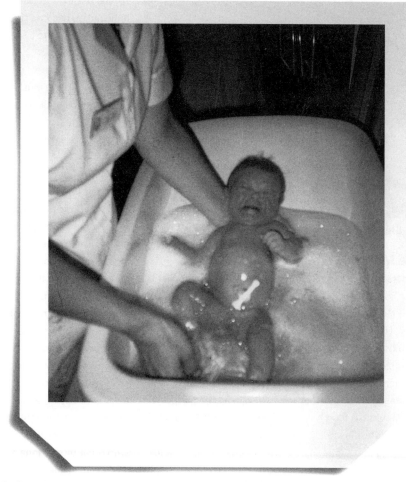

The last thing I wanted to do was watch the child being bathed

was lagging well behind at the moment. Where was God's love in this? Steve seemed not to hear a word Paul said, he just sat there looking stunned.

Heidi has a special friendship with Pastor Paul

The Man from the Ministry

"Hello Heidi, it's morning time'. Heidi is very good in the mornings. Unlike some other children we could mention, she isn't prone to wandering around in the small hours (well, six o'clock) whistling or slamming doors. She sits quietly in her bed looking at books until one of us goes to her. She looks up with a huge grin, delighted to see me and excited at the prospect of another great day.

'Hello my friend, what day is it today?'

'Sunday.'

'Yay! Sunday today we go to church and learn about God and Jesus and see Uncle PAUL!'

Heidi has had a special friendship with Pastor Paul from that first day of her life when he held her and loved her. Of course, being a Pastor, Paul has no favourites. All the lambs in his flock are equal, but an observer could be forgiven for thinking that one is more equal than others.

One Sunday we had a special sense of anticipation because three young people were to be baptised.

'There will be lots of visitors today. We must get there in good time or there won't be any seats.'

Liz was always trying to get the rest of us organised, but once again our noble intention of punctuality did not quite work out as intended. We arrived just in time and Liz went straight into the church with the other children. Heidi, true to form, chose this moment to ask for the toilet, leaving me stranded. It is always a struggle to chivvy along a child who insists on helping to flush the toilet (once is never enough) and wash and dry her hands with great thoroughness.

Somewhat less calmly than planned, we walked in the door, her hand tightly held in mine—a lesson learnt through past experience. A surprise was in store; the whole congregation was facing towards us. I soon realised that Heidi was delighted with the new arrangement. It meant she could see all her friends, and plenty more nice people who no doubt soon would be her friends.

'Hello Uncle Paul' (waving to the Pastor and receiving an answering grin), 'hello Aunty Eunice, hello Aunty Ruth'. I was frantically scanning the sea of faces. Where was Liz? Had she hidden in embarrassment and left me to it?

'Hello Tizzy, hello Baby Ham'. (As soon as he was born Heidi had decided this was a far better name than Abraham). I dragged Heidi's arm back towards me as she made her way along the row to give him a warmer greeting than a simple hello.

'Hello Uncle David, hello Uncle Martin'. I realised that the entire congregation, with the exception of myself,

seemed to find this grand entrance highly amusing. At last I saw Liz waving from the back row. I dragged the chubby little hand squashed in my sweating palm, and the rest of Heidi trailed protestingly behind. I sank gratefully into my seat.

Later, Liz apologised to Pastor Paul, hoping that his preparation for the service had not been disturbed too much. 'Oh no', was his reply, 'I had been feeling quite tense, but I felt far more relaxed after that!' So the episode became another example of Heidi's unique ability to make everyone apart from her parents feel at ease.

Some months later Heidi again had an encouraging word for the pastor before the service. This time he was in the cloakroom when we made our usual pre-service visit, preparing himself before the mirror.

'Hello Uncle Paul', said Heidi delightedly. But once ensconced in the cubicle,

she peered round the door and pronounced severely, 'You've been a very naughty boy!'

'Oh dear, what have I done?'

'You must go out at once', she decreed, neatly side-stepping the question.

'But I must make myself look at least a bit respectable', the miscreant protested weakly. The little face peered round the corner again to weigh up this mitigation, and changed tack.

'You look very pretty', she encouraged, and Pastor went off to lead the service with his self esteem suitably buoyed.

One Sunday we were delighted to be invited to the Pastor's house for dinner and tea. If our pleasure may have been partially due to the prospect of a day free of food preparation, the children's was entirely because of the improved company. Heidi's attachment to Uncle Paul and Aunty Hazel is only rivalled by her love of Monty, their amazingly longsuffering collie. He must groan inwardly at the sight of her, but outwardly conducts himself with admirable restraint. Immediately Heidi was in the garden throwing a ball for him to chase. It wasn't terribly exciting for him, since the ball never travelled more than a couple of metres if it failed to hit him full on. She roared with glee every time he faithfully brought it back, adding a running commentary as excitedly as any horse racing commentator: 'He's chasin' the ball, he's got it now, he's eatin' the ball!'

Since Monty didn't sit up to dinner, Heidi then had to entertain herself with lesser mortals. Once she had made sure she had everything she wanted to eat, she decided to impress herself on the conversation. She turned to her seventy year old neighbour (Heidi hasn't heard of the generation gap):

'Peter'ogan, d'you like meat? Do you? Do you?' To Heidi the delicious roast beef was lumped under the same generic term as Spam and beefburgers. 'I like meat too. D'you like carrots?'

'I like carrots', a sibling managed to interject, but Heidi was not to be deflected from her task.

'D'you like soup? Do you?'

'What kind of soup?'

'Egg'

'I've never heard of egg soup'

'I like soup. Tim likes soup.' Turning towards the other end of the table: 'D'you like soup?' It was beginning to feel like a cross between the Spanish inquisition and a market research survey. 'Peter'ogan, d'you like Cheerios? '

'Yes, I do'

'I don't like Cheerios. Tim doesn't like Cheerios. Daniel likes Cheerios'...

Eventually Heidi was satisfied that our dietary preferences had been sufficiently well aired. Her attention returned to her 'meat'.

After this episode Heidi would regularly speak to Monty on her toy phone:

'Hello Monty, how are you? Are you playing in the garden with your ball? Did you fall in the pond? Okay. Goodbye.'

He was also faithfully remembered in her prayers, and we were reliably informed that he kept in very good health. Unfortunately Monty's promotion was at the expense of Pastor Paul, so we were grateful not to notice any deterioration in the quality of his sermons.

A hard day's night

 The staff did all they could to help us. I soon told them I couldn't face being in a ward full of other mums with their perfect babies and we were given a room of our own. I was less pleased when I saw they had put the baby's cot between our beds. I didn't even want her in the room, let alone dividing us, depriving us of the grain of comfort and strength we would derive from sharing our grief in each other's arms. We soon banished her cot to the corner and pushed the beds together.

We forced ourselves to find the Gideon Bible and read Psalm 139, though I felt really angry with God. Why me? I was only twenty-eight! One section grabbed my corkscrewing mind and held it still, though I could not embrace the depth of its truths at the time:

'For you created my inmost being; you knit me together in my mother's womb. I praise you because I am fearfully and wonderfully made; your works are wonderful, I know that full well. My frame was not hidden from you when I was made in the secret place. When I was woven together in the depths of the earth, your eyes saw my unformed body. All the days ordained for me were written in your book before one of them came to be.'

Despite myself, I knew at that moment that one day I would be able to accept Heidi for the person she was. Whether it would be days, months or years I had no idea. But ultimately I too would cherish this person whom her Creator valued so highly.

 We lay in the darkness as the hospital continued its ceaseless activity beyond the door of our room. Nearby the production line of healthy babies continued unabated as we shared our sorrow and mourned our failure to achieve the expected result. *Born on the Third of July—Loss of Independence Day*, I thought to myself with extremely black humour.

Physically and mentally empty, our minds stubbornly refused to slow down as we sought respite. How could we encourage each other when we were both at our lowest point? I could think of only one thing which might alleviate Liz's pain by even a degree: 'Heidi doesn't have to be the last one now'.

Steve's words hung in my brain as I tried to focus on the pinprick of light they contained. Yet even as I did so I felt guilt; my handicapped daughter was just a few hours old and already I wanted to replace her with the complete version. My thoughts spun and twisted with my body as I tried unsuccessfully to rest. This day had so nearly been one of the best of my life, yet had turned out to be the worst. I grieved with a depth I had never known for the daughter I had lost.

 Poor Heidi, she'll never be like the boys, full of life and intelligence, independent, self-assured. She won't have boyfriends or marry or have children. I'll never be able to do her hair in pretty plaits with bows because Down's children always have pudding basin hairstyles. No chance of her going to university, or being a nurse or teacher. It's so sad. God, why have you done this?

I felt Steve against me, his body racked with sobs. I was pleased that he was releasing some of that flood of emotion; grief, anger, pain that was threatening to overwhelm us. Yet I felt so helpless. *Why couldn't I give him the daughter he wanted? Is it my fault? Have I committed some terrible sin and God is punishing me? How will I cope? I've got a three year old and an eighteen month old and now this girl who will need so much extra help and attention. All those hospital appointments she'll have, and she's bound to have other medical problems...Down's children are more prone to so many illnesses. God, I can't do it, I just can't take it...*

Finally exhaustion had its way and I slept a little. Frequently through that long, long night I would wake again to that dreadful feeling that something was terribly wrong...oh yes, I would remember, and my mind would begin again its tortured repetitive journey.

No joy in the morning

The new day dragged round eventually; the first day of the rest of my suddenly turned upside-down life. Often problems that have loomed so threateningly during a disturbed night seem far more manageable in the light of day, but not this one. As I shuffled gingerly along the corridor I contemplated the prospect of being visited by friends. This usually gave me a sense of pleasurable anticipation, but today I didn't want to see anyone. I knew they wouldn't know what to say to me. I just hoped they wouldn't trot out the usual stereotypical platitudes about people with Down's: 'They're very affectionate and always happy,' or 'People say they're very placid', or 'They love music, don't they'. They would mean well, but it was the last sort of thing I wanted to hear. Although stereotypes usually have some basis in fact, they invariably present a simplistic picture, like my stupid thought in the night about pudding basins. I knew already from my past experience that children with Down's can be stubborn, wilful and exhausting, just like any other child. The sound of babies crying assaulted my senses as I limped past the nursery. How I wished I could swap Heidi for one of them.

I even dreaded seeing my boys. When they charged in, exuding energy and excitement, talking non-stop, it only served to emphasise what I thought I had lost. As she lay there so weak and tiny I couldn't believe Heidi would ever be like her brothers. They were desperate to cuddle her and gave her up with great reluctance. They posed delightedly with her and us for photos. Their smiles were the only ones which were a true reflection of inner feelings. It upset me still more to see their unconditional love; they loved her because she was theirs. They clearly felt she was gorgeous. I wanted to love her as they did, but I couldn't accept her for the person she was. They didn't notice her Down's syndrome, whereas it was the only thing I could think about.

The nurses brought us some booklets full of information about Down's syndrome. I didn't want to take this step along the road to reality, but forced myself to pick one up. 'Your Baby Has Down's Syndrome', announced the cover, as if I didn't know. 'You probably feel sorrow…anger…shock…guilt.' *You're not wrong there.* 'About one in 1000 babies is born with Down's syndrome'. *So why does it have to be mine? Things like this don't happen to me; I'm one of the 999.* The God in whom I believed was a wise, loving King in total control of his universe and all his people. There were no probabilities or mistakes, no such thing as bad luck. All the events of my life were in his perfect will. It was a good theory, but at this moment I didn't like the practice of it one little bit. *It's so unfair!*

'Down's syndrome is caused by an extra chromosome number 21, making 47 in all…your baby may have delayed development…looser muscles and joints…slower weight gain…eyes that slant…a flatter than average head…a single crease across the palm…' *All that just from one stupid extra chromosome.* '…prone to chest and sinus infections…feeding problems…the body's heat-regulating mechanism does not always work well…your baby's skin may be very dry…particular attention to help control her tongue…about one in three children born with Down's syndrome has a heart defect…' *Are they more susceptible to every health problem? As if she won't have enough to cope with! Still, at least the doctor said her heart seemed all right.* Actually, I admitted grudgingly to myself, the booklet was honest and helpful. I'd homed in on the bad news bits because of the negativity within me.

I tossed it aside and picked up a glossy little book called *Just Kids,* full of beautiful pictures of children with Down's syndrome. Although many had been through various health problems, I was surprised and impressed by some of their achievements: 'Stacey was walking unaided at thirteen months', 'Amy is two, says eight to ten words and understands nearly everything', 'Helen entered mainstream infant school at five'. Yet I was still sceptical, and when the nurse who had brought the literature came back I asked if these children were typical, or had they picked out the best ones to try and cheer new parents up. 'Lots of them do very well nowadays', she replied. 'Far more is done than before to help them realise their potential'. Maybe our future hadn't been wrecked quite so comprehensively as I'd thought.

Her brothers clearly felt she was gorgeous

My parents arrived that afternoon. They always dropped everything and rushed with great excitement to see a new grandchild. Heidi was number thirteen, but unlike any of the first twelve. I hadn't even been looking forward to seeing them this time. They looked shell-shocked, but tried to be positive for our sake. 'Isn't she beautiful!', my mum said as she cuddled Heidi. I felt like yelling 'No she isn't, can't you see she's got Down's syndrome?'

 A doctor came later to take some blood for the test that would prove what we already knew. A simple procedure, you might think, but not with Heidi. She appeared to have no blood at all in one foot, so when the doctor could find nowhere else to stick her pin she abandoned it, bruised and flaming, and turned to the other. The resistance of this one was finally broken and it grudgingly yielded sufficient to satisfy its tormentor. 'But not with Heidi' was to become a familiar mantra as every little thing became fraught with unexpected complications.

We were trying to recover from this ordeal when the consultant came in to check Heidi over himself. Then he passed the stethoscope to the student who had accompanied him. 'What do you think?' But he had to help her out. 'Would you say the second beat is a bit loud?' Then he turned to us. 'I don't think it's anything to worry about, but I'd like you to bring her back for an echocardiogram. That's an ultrasound scan on her heart'. Maybe nothing for him to worry about, I thought.

Home alone

 Only the day before we'd come this way so full of anticipation. Now we returned, subdued by the presence of the little burden wrapped in blankets in an attempt to keep her floppy body upright in her seat. Another psychological step; it was just us now. Yes, there will be lots of help from the community health team and family and friends. But really we're on our own. Panic rose within me. *I can't cope...I wish Jesus would come again right now so I don't have to be a parent any more. What a terrible thought; now that's something else to feel guilty about...*

 Soon cards and letters began to arrive; first a trickle and then a flow that continued for the next couple of weeks and beyond. Many were from people we hardly knew, but over a hundred cared enough to write, from a simple thought to a three page letter. As we struggled with our fluctuating feelings we felt supported on this tide of love and carefully-chosen words. Several came from people who had been through similar experiences and brought hope that there could be a brighter future.

'A special welcome to little Heidi Anne. May you be given that special grace that will enable you to fully surrender to our loving Heavenly Father, and be able to accept the little child as a special gift from his hand, albeit through tears'.

Yes, that was just what we wanted to do, but it was so hard. From deep within we were fighting against God's disruption of our plans for our life. God's grace was indeed the only antidote to this. It was a common thread in these messages. Another theme was the truth of God's loving control of all the circumstances of our lives. It was never expressed in a glib way which had no thought for the pain of our present experience. Several quoted from a poem called *The Divine Weaver*:

Man's life is laid in the loom of time
To a pattern he does not see,
While the weaver works and the shuttles fly
Till the end of eternity.

Some shuttles are filled with silver thread,
And some with threads of gold;
While often but the darker hue
Is all that they may hold.

But the weaver watches with skilful eye
Each shuttle fly to and fro,
And sees the pattern so deftly wrought
As the loom works sure and slow.

God surely planned that pattern
Each thread—the dark and the fair—
Was chosen by his master skill
And placed in the web with care.

He only knows the beauty
And guides the shuttles which hold
The threads so unattractive,
As well as the threads of gold.

Not till the loom is silent
And the shuttles cease to fly,
Shall God unroll the canvas
And explain the reason why

The dark threads are as needful
In the weaver's skilful hand
As the threads of gold and silver
In the pattern he has planned.

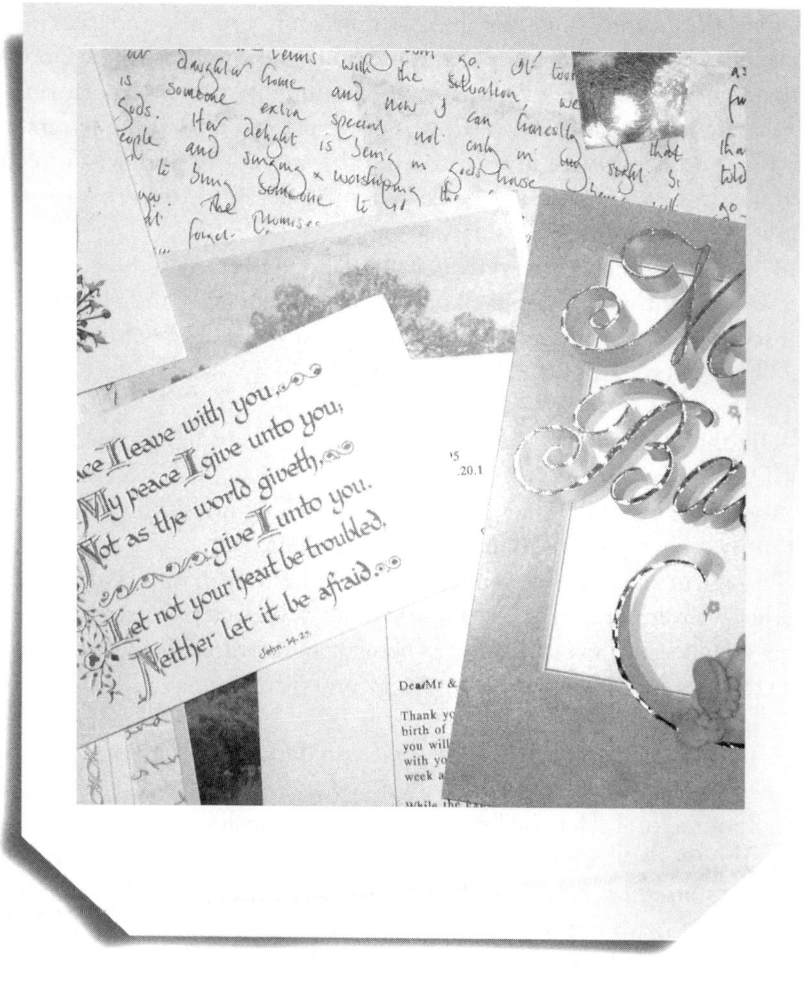

Over a hundred people cared enough to write

The tangled mess of dark threads on our underside view was so real and immediate it seemed impossible to believe there was a beautiful tapestry being created on God's side, though our heads knew it was indeed a wonderful truth.

'Our prayers are night and day embracing you all, and seeking to commit you all into the hands of our gracious and compassionate God and Father, who has infinite wisdom to direct, almighty power to perform and everlasting love to comfort.' Dad was not that keen on writing letters, but those he did send were always treasured for the love and wisdom they contained. It was striking how many others also told us of their commitment to pray for us every day.

Before long Janet, a friend from church, popped in.

'We thought you might like some help with cooking and cleaning and that sort of thing', she said. 'How often would you like one of us to come?'

'That's very thoughtful,' Liz replied. 'Once a week would be a great help.'

'Oh, that's not much. We've got enough people to have someone every day if you'd like it'.

And come every day they did from a church of under thirty members, faithfully relieving Liz of many everyday burdens.

Though in one sense we were going through the deep waters alone, yet in another we were supported by a marvellous web given great strength by its many strands. The love of Jesus was being demonstrated in all sorts of ways from the deeply spiritual to the intensely practical.

'I'm more than happy to come up if you'd like to talk things over', my brother was saying.

'Thanks a lot. I'll let you know'. I put the phone down.

Hmm. It's very good of him to offer to travel from London. But Pastor Paul said something similar only the other day. Strange, this sudden desire for my company. I haven't turned into Moses or Elijah overnight, so they must be worried about me. They must think I'm bottling up the emotion of this whole situation.

Perhaps they are right. Am I turning all the anger and sadness on myself so that it is becoming destructive to me? I would be happy to talk to either of them at greater length and depth than I have done. I may do at some stage. I just don't feel the need at the moment. Perhaps it's just me. I'm not one of these people who need to talk and talk and talk about things. I'm often happy just to work things through in my own mind. Is that weird? I wonder if other people are like that. Perhaps I'm an emotional pygmy. I know I can be an unsociable so-and-so, Liz has told me that plenty of times. Anyway, Liz is certainly one of those people who need to talk and talk and talk about things, so I talk it through endlessly with her. And we can share the things we wouldn't be able to say to anyone else. That certainly helps both of us. We're going through it. We understand. With the best will in the world, I'm not sure a person who hadn't experienced something similar would really be able to empathise. Maybe someone would, but I'd rather not take the risk if I don't need to. I wouldn't want to bare my soul and end up just feeling naked.

 We borrowed a daunting academic-looking book from the library. It was a bit old, and full of depressing studies and statistics about Down's syndrome and the progress, or lack of it, we could expect Heidi to make. It made for masochistic reading, but we wanted to know as much as possible. One particular statistic leapt from the the page in true cliché style: 'Around 25% of babies born with Down's syndrome die in infancy.' 25%! Maybe the book was a bit out of date, but I had no idea the figure would be that high. I was revolted by the mixed feelings this piece of information engendered within me. I would never have imagined myself capable of such thoughts before, nor would I expect anyone who has not been in a similar position to understand. But suddenly there before me was the alluring prospect of wiping this disastrous unrehearsed scene from my play and reverting to the original script.

Yet there before me lay my helpless daughter whom I was betraying.

Steve soon had to be back at work; being self-employed meant any paternity leave was self-awarded and usually only lasted a day at best. Still, it did have advantages; working from home he was at least around some of the time. Not that I was left alone with my thoughts; both sets of parents and my sister stayed in turns to help.

My thoughts, though, would not be thwarted. My struggle to accept Heidi was by no means won. I wished I knew how severely she would be affected. Down's syndrome always carries with it a degree of physical and learning disability, but I had seen a huge variation in the people I had known. Would she be like my cousin, who never sat up during the three years of her life, or like the girl whose picture I had seen recently in the local paper, flushed with achievement as she gleefully ripped up her 'L' plates? It shouldn't make any difference, I knew that, but it would be so much easier to accept her if I knew that her faculties would only be a little impaired. I wanted to know the future, but God in his wisdom has chosen to withhold from his creation that aspect of his being. In effect I was wanting to steal a slice of his 'Godness'. I was gazing longingly at the same forbidden fruit Adam and Eve had been unable to resist. I had to accept the present and trust God for whatever the future might hold. But I couldn't help wondering. God's perspective was unconstrained by human limitations. What could he see…

Close encounters of the absurd kind

As Heidi began to talk her streak of imaginative independence was soon shining through. One of her first words was 'Daniel', but she refused to say 'Tim', which you would have thought was easier. This made Tim rather sad. Then she decided he would be called 'Bill'.

'Heidi, it's Tim'.

'No, 'e Bill.' After a number of such exchanges, we realised she was not making a mistake but was adamant she would call him what she wanted. Tim was delighted she had made up her own name for him and happily played along with it. We soon found she could say 'Tim' perfectly well when she occasionally slipped up and quickly corrected herself.

Heidi's great friend Aunty Eunice, a retired lady who regularly looked after her, was suddenly christened 'Cookie'. For months it was all Heidi would call her, no doubt with some good reason that she kept hidden from the rest of us.

Liz was given the title 'My mummy darlin'' and for my part I was most gratified with the respectful form of address she adopted for me. Unfortunately calling me 'My daddy Sir' seemed to have little impact on the rest of her behaviour. Eventually she graduated to the more familiar 'My friend'.

A development of this habit was role-playing with the others.

'I'm LaLa and you're Tinky Winky'. Or, when we hired a Chucklevision-style four wheeled bike on holiday, it was 'I'm Barry and you're Paul.'

Barely a day goes by without having the house full of Woody and Buzz Lightyear, mother and baby, lion and tiger. Heidi immerses herself fully in her role:

'Heidi, what would you like on your bread?'

'I'm not Heidi', she retorts crossly. 'I'm Monty the dog.'

'Monty, what would you like on your bread?'

'Chocolate spread please,' comes the happy reply.

Sometimes she will give the wrong answer to a question just to make it more interesting.

'Have you got brothers?'

'No', provoking the required surprised reaction.

'I've got boys.'

'What are their names?' She casts her eye round the room for inspiration, until it lights on a lurid pink talking toy.

'Barney.'

'Barney?'

'Yes. Barney Dan and Barney Tim.' She bursts into peals of laughter at her joke.

Her alternative sense of humour keeps us all amused and is another evidence of her individual character. She rushes off behind the settee, yelling as she goes:

'Don't chase me, you fruit pastille!'

Heidi loves any new experience. She was hugely excited to discover soon after her fifth birthday that we had a holiday booked. The boys bore the agonising countdown with stoicism, but Heidi's concept of delay doesn't stretch beyond 'wait a minute'; and her minutes are about ten seconds long. So each day she would announce at breakfast time 'We're going on holiday today. We're going to Majorca in an aeroplane'. Our efforts to persuade her that our departure was not that imminent were met with an unshakeable 'Yes we ARE going on holiday today. We're going to Majorca in an aeroplane.' Once Heidi's mind is made up there is not much point arguing, so we gradually gave up. However, she never seemed disappointed to reach the end of another day and find we were still here. Each day for her is a pleasure she enjoys to the full, so I suppose she didn't really mind. The next morning she would utter her mantra with undimmed confidence.

One breakfast time we were finally able to say 'Yes, we are!' and the children took up an impatient vigil for the taxi to the airport. The driver rolled his eyes and grinned wryly.

'You're taking that lot with you?' I discovered on the way that he spent half the year in his native Jamaica, so I guess two weeks in Majorca with kids wasn't a prospect likely to provoke too great a degree of envy.

Journeys out were not a huge success. Having enjoyed the peaceful charm of Minorca the previous year, Majorca in August resembled a huge anthill. Its beauty was hidden beneath a layer of crawling tourists laden with ten times their weight in cameras, camcorders and guide books. Beaches were more popular, although not all the neighbouring children appreciated Heidi's efforts to help with their sandcastles. But the most popular activities were on site.

'Let's go to the 'wimmin' pool', Heidi would proclaim, 'and play with my friends again.' Heidi's friends were any other children who happened to be there. Her favourite activity was ducking Germans. I tried to explain to her that there was no need for this sort of thing any more, since we had actually beaten Germany the last time we had played football, but to no avail. In any case, they seemed to find her very amusing.

The kids' clubs were also popular, with the children as well as us; and the staff always seemed delighted to see Heidi especially, despite the extra angst she caused them. One time I was regretfully wending my way to collect the girls at the end of peacetime when I found Heidi making her way determinedly in the direction of the swimming pool, having sneaked out past the doorkeeper. She does make the most of her lack of stature in whatever ways she can.

Heidi came up with various catch phrases during the holiday. The first she picked up from the club; and every time she thought we should be going out she would holler 'Are we all READY?' With children who struggle to remember themselves, let alone all the other paraphernalia, this pronouncement was often made repeatedly and with increasing impatience before we actually left.

Whenever she knocked her drink over, or drew on someone else's picture, or squirted sun cream on the floor, Heidi would exclaim 'Whoops! I did it again!' and grin round delightedly at everyone. This attempt to disarm any possible retribution for her latest misdemeanour was usually very successful. One time she was being rebuked she suddenly came out with 'Shut your big fat gob!' She was most gratified with the response this one got and proceeded to use it on every possible occasion. Eventually we managed to control ourselves enough to tell her with a straight face that this was not the sort of thing to say. Thereafter she just murmured it to the other children when she thought we weren't listening. Hypocritically, she was always keen to back up our disciplining of the others. If anyone dared to dispute an accusation of wrongdoing she would call out 'Yes you did, I saw yer!' as reliably as any hired witness.

 Flying home, Heidi is supposed to be going to sleep, but is still full of irrepressible life. Finally exhausted, she shuts her eyes. I smile down at the peaceful face in my lap.

Thank you, Lord, for this little package of joy. But what about the next five years? School soon, how will she cope? Will she get left out, or left behind? What if she's ill again? Oh no, I'm at it again, trying to grab the fruit. It's easier to accept the present now, but I don't know about the next five years…or five months, or five weeks. I still need to trust God for whatever the future might hold.

Chapter 5

Stepping out

 At times dark impulses would rise unbidden from within me...if we had a car accident and somebody had to die, I would want it to be Heidi... This only added to my anguish. I felt almost overwhelmed with guilt because I could not yet see Heidi as being of equal value to the others.

At other moments I would become defiant; I wasn't going to give in to this. Everyone would expect Heidi to be a failure by all the measurements of success our society used. Well, she wasn't going to be. She would walk early and talk young and get GCSE's and go to university...maybe. I marched downstairs and announced 'She's going to be the best Down's child ever.'

Steve looked at me calmly. 'We'll help her to be the best she can be.'

He was infuriatingly right, of course. Comparing, comparing, it was so hard to get out of that mindset. I had to accept her as an individual and do my best for her, whatever her limitations might be.

I was determined to take Daniel to playgroup myself before term finished that week. Having the ordeal of facing the other mums and playgroup helpers hanging over me all summer would be worse than actually doing it, so I was going to get it over with.

'You must send her here—we've never had a child with Down's and we'd love to have her'. It was the best thing the playgroup leader could have said and I went home feeling a little encouraged.

Another big step was the first time out at church. I was dreading someone innocently saying the wrong thing, which wouldn't be difficult, and my sharp retort shooting out before I could grab it. A wise friend from church advised me not to try to answer people who made ill-informed comments about Down's syndrome. 'Just smile and say thank you.' She knew me well enough to realise I might otherwise bite some innocent head off and have something else to feel guilty about. And then there was William, born two weeks before Heidi. He had looked like a three month old when he was born. I didn't even want to look at him, even bigger now, healthy and perfect. I didn't know how I would bear it, but it had to be faced.

'*Hymn number 320*'. *Oh great,* I thought sarcastically, *I know what that is.*

'God moves in a mysterious way…' *Well, that's true enough.* The tears streamed unchecked down my cheeks as the singing continued in the distance.

> 'His purposes will ripen fast,
>   Unfolding every hour;
> The bud may have a bitter taste,
>   But sweet will be the flower'.

There was no doubting the bitterness of the bud; but could there really be a sweet flower? I was trying to reach into the future again, and it looked very dark.

A view with a bloom

The reality was that the future had looked dark because my short-sighted eyes could not see beyond the dark present. But the bud gradually opened.

On good days we have one child with special needs. On bad days it feels as though we have several, and the unfashionable expression 'slow learner' sometimes seems more appropriate for the others. Especially when it comes to table manners. Complex tasks such as getting more dinner in the mouth than down the shirt; or avoiding the stick-your-finger-in-the-jam-lick-it-then-do-it-again technique. Their progress often seems inversely proportional to their age. This is rather a damning indictment of our parenting skills. It becomes depressing after repeated exposure to the harsh realities of the Crowter mealtime.

After one particularly harrowing dinner we were both feeling frazzled. Heidi decided it was an appropriate moment to stretch our fizzing nerve ends a little further. Parents of children with Down's are often rather sensitive about them exhibiting stereotypical mannerisms or forms of behaviour and we are no exception. So when Heidi lolled her tongue out provocatively, I said sternly 'Put that tongue away. We don't want to see it!'

The offending appendage immediately popped back inside. 'Okay' said Heidi, with her usual obliging response. The problem is that the next response is usually less obliging. It gradually slid back out again. 'Less lee **goo** lont to shlee it', she said. (Sorry if you can't understand her, but it's rather difficult to grin, stick your tongue out and talk at the same time—you try it). When she realised we were dismally failing to hold our straight faces she burst into delighted laughter. We gave up and joined in.

'Show-off!', she said, which, assuming she meant herself, was quite accurate. 'Let's all have a dance!'

Due to Heidi's highly effective stress-relieving technique we felt more like dancing than we had a couple of minutes earlier.

After dinner each evening (this is the aim, at least) we have Bible Time with the children. This consists of a short interactive Bible story, prayers and songs. Heidi is very fond of songs with actions. As soon as she was old enough to participate in Bible Time she would join in enthusiastically with these and the few words she remembered. She would choose 'The wise man built his house upon the rock' or 'Only a boy called David' for days on end until the rest of us were heartily sick of them. One day she decided she wanted a turn at praying. Being Heidi, she wasn't content with a one sentence effort to break herself in gently, but went straight for the ministerial style; in length if not depth. She tended to mention whatever entered her head, which caused great difficulty for the boys (and their parents) in trying not to laugh, especially as Heidi would look round all the while, checking our reaction and searching for inspiration for the next line. When she ran out of ideas she would start all over again, until one of us intervened with an 'Amen'.

On a visit to my brother, Heidi rather apprehensively made the acquaintance of Sparky, the family budgie. For some time after this she prayed for him every night, and if anyone dared to pray for another member of the family she would add 'and Sparky!' in a piercing whisper.

When one or more of the children had fallen foul of us, which was not infrequent, Heidi rarely missed the opportunity to bring this into her prayers:

'Daniel's been naughty. Help Daniel be good. Tim's been naughty. Help Tim be good.' But, despite our joggings of her conscience, at this stage she never felt the need to include herself in this time of confession.

Sometimes she would seem to be in a reasonably sensible mood and start well, before straying into the realms of fantasy:

'Please help mummy's poorly back get better soon. Please help Robert 'Ardman get poorly.' (we put this down to a slip of the tongue). 'Please help the Lord Mayor and the nightmare.' By now we were manfully stifling giggles behind our hands. The Lord Mayor had been to her school the previous week; presumably she thought the nightmare was some relation. 'Help the Lord Mayor in the hall. Help the Lord Mayor shake our hands. Help the nightmare. Amen'. We gratefully moved on to Daniel, who made the unwise move of issuing a correction by praying that Robert Hardman would get better.

'No, get POORLY' came Heidi's indignant whisper. Liz had just managed to compose herself and her prayer was in full flow when Heidi interjected 'Pray for Jigglypuff!' (For the uninitiated, Jigglypuff is a Pokemon). At this stage we belatedly decided this particular Bible Time was beyond redemption.

Once the novelty of her idiosyncratic style had worn off we were less prone to fits of giggles and were able to appreciate the growing thoughtfulness behind her prayers. She would often pray for people who were ill, remembering from earlier conversations or previous days. As her understanding developed she demonstrated surprising sensitivity and insight for a child with such limitations. Her contributions became a valued part of Bible Time.

Our flower was gradually emerging, revealing more layers of vibrant colour.

Chapter 6

The shape of things to come

 We had all the usual postnatal visits from midwives, health visitors and so on. These were more frequent than on previous occasions and always lasted much longer as each one had their pennyworth of wisdom to offer. Some were worth far more than their face value; others rather less. On day nine our first non-standard visitor sprang onto the doorstep, large as life and twice as bubbly.

'Hello, I'm Kate, darling. I'm going to be Heidi's physiotherapist.' Some months later we found out that she was known as Kate Darling as this was her standard form of greeting. Within five minutes we knew all about her. We were delighted to find that she was a Christian and she was quite over the moon to discover that we were too. When she bounced out about an hour later we felt slightly less down than our normal still very low level. This was our first contact with the excellent service we would receive from the special needs community health and education team, and within a day or two we had the second. A car drew up and an elegant raven-haired woman emerged.

'Just popping in to introduce myself. I'll be seeing a lot of you because I'll be Heidi's teacher.' *What does Heidi need a teacher for,* I wondered. *You don't usually have one of them until you're four or five.*

'I'll see her about once a week when term starts.' Since it was the summer holiday Carole had come to see us in her own time. The years ahead would prove this extra effort was typical of her commitment to Heidi; and also the usefulness of having a teacher when you are two months old.

 July 13th, time to go back to hospital for that echocardiogram. I hoped Steve would be free to come with me; he rarely knew until the morning whether he would need to be out buying cars that day. I wondered whether he really wanted to come.

We sat waiting in the bare corridor. I was so relieved to have Steve with me, yet apprehensive about what we may be about to find out. Then we were in, Heidi lying on her back, cold jelly smeared over her chest, uncomplaining as usual. We peered attentively at the swirling colours on the monitor as the doctor moved the sensor, though the picture meant nothing to us. Finally she spoke. 'Heidi does have a small hole in her heart. It's nothing serious. It may heal of its own accord or she might need an operation, but not until she's two or three.' *Oh no, she has got a heart problem as well as everything else…at least it's not a bad one…she said it's not serious…but I had hoped it would be all OK…*

The result of the Down's syndrome blood test had come through too. When I heard it I realised that somewhere deep I had been clinging to the last gossamer thread that the last ten days had all been a ghastly mistake.

A mother from the local Down's group contacted me. It was good to talk to someone who had been through the same situation and come out positively on the other side.

'You may feel it's too early for you to cope with, but we have got a meeting this week. You're very welcome to come if you'd like to.'

I oscillated back and forth over the next few days. It would be good to meet more parents and they might have some helpful suggestions; but would my emotions be up to it? I fought the fear and summoned the courage to go.

There were about five mums there. After a while the conversation turned to their children.

'I'm having real problems with getting George dry at night. He's seven now, but just can't seem to get the hang of it'.

'I had the same with John. He's just about got it now. For ages I had to get up in the night to put him on the toilet'.

'How old is John?' I asked nervously.

'He's nine.'

I felt a growing panic. These were things I was going through with my three year old. Would I still be suffering them with Heidi when she was nine? It was clearly quite natural to the others, they were used to it; but to me it was a new and depressing line of thought.

'How does he get on at school?' I asked, trying to move the subject away from the various behavioural problems they were discussing. This was another mistake, as I soon discovered they all went to special schools. So much for increased integration into mainstream education. It didn't seem to be happening here; was it all just hype? I didn't want Heidi to be bussed off to another school, I wanted her to go with the boys, as far as possible to be like other children. But it looked as though it didn't happen; perhaps mainstream schools wouldn't have them when it came to it.

'I was stupid to go to a meeting so soon', I thought angrily as I returned home; the future seemingly laid out hopelessly before me.

Heart of the matter

 In many ways Heidi was a model baby, contented and happy enough to feed. She didn't wake much at night and slept quite a bit in the daytime too. She was slow to gain weight but we weren't too worried as we knew this was common in babies with Down's syndrome. July 23rd was the red letter day when the midwife's measurement showed she had regained her birth weight.

Eight days later I took her to the consultant for a routine four week check. He found she had slipped well below her birth weight again. He seemed very concerned about her purple hands and feet, which we were used to, and her breathlessness, which seemed worse.

'I'd like her to go to Birmingham Children's Hospital tomorrow'. Immediately my heart and mind were racing. *To the specialist centre, and so urgently…it must be very serious.* Too overcome with the sudden shock to take in what he said, I sat crying as his words danced round my head. Arriving home still dazed, I blurted it out to two of my faithful friends who had been looking after the boys, and doing my housework, while I was at the appointment. Steve was sixty miles away, so they stayed for the next hour or so, lending support at a very vulnerable point.

A little later, Janet called with a ready-cooked meal for us, unaware of the day's development. By now my brain had arranged the doctor's dancing words into some semblance of order, and the questions I had been unable to form at the time were crystallising in my mind. So Janet, being a doctor, was an ideal visitor at that moment. It was a great help to be able to talk things through with her. Only a little thing, easily dismissed as coincidence, but to me another fleeting glimpse of God's hand.

One scrap of the encounter I had recalled was the doctor saying to a colleague that her liver and spleen were enlarged. I now found my worst fears confirmed; this was a sign of heart failure.

The next morning we sat in the scanning room at Birmingham watching with a familiar feeling of trepidation as the sensor was placed on Heidi's chest. What would be the interpretation of the pulsating kaleidoscope of colours this time?

Finally we heard a diagnosis with vastly different implications to the previous one. Yes, there was a hole in her heart, but it was certainly not a minor one that wouldn't affect her much.

'The heart has two collecting chambers (atria) and two pumping chambers (ventricles)', the heart consultant explained patiently. 'They should be separated by a wall (septum) and valves, but Heidi's heart has a large hole in the middle causing massive leakage. It's called an Atrio Ventricular Septal Defect because the hole straddles both the atria and the ventricles, so there is leakage across all four areas. This is putting a great strain on her heart and lungs which will cause them to fail completely before very long.

'She will need an operation to repair the hole. However, she is not strong enough yet; we would like to wait until she is four or five months old if we can. At the moment all her energy is going into keeping her heart going which is why she is not gaining weight. We will put her on a constant tube feed with energy supplements. She'll need to have the operation before she is six months old or I'm afraid you'll lose her.'

Our minds were reeling once again, disorientated as we tried to absorb the impact of this latest punch to the head. Mixed with the shock and sadness was anger and disbelief; how could the previous diagnosis have been so different? It would be hard to have confidence again in the local hospital. Yet we were also thankful that this life-threatening condition had been found in time; and we were now sure that Heidi was in the best hands.

 The best place it was, convenient it certainly was not. The twenty mile separation from home was an additional stress on us. One application point of this pressure was on my determination to keep breast feeding Heidi for as long as possible. I had believed it was best for the boys. It was a kind of symbol of my resolve to do my best for Heidi and treat her in the same way as them. The closest I could get to this now was to express my milk to go in Heidi's feeding tube. This entailed staying at the hospital more or less twenty-four hours a day. We slept in a room next to the ward and Steve commuted home to work each day. Our helpers went into overdrive looking after the boys, cooking, ironing, cleaning more than ever. I was glad when other parents at the hospital gave me the opportunity to tell them about this as it presented such a positive image of what a church family should be like. But I felt pulled in two directions, like a piece of elastic stretched taut. I wanted to be near Heidi; I hated abandoning her helpless and alone in her cot. Yet I felt guilty that I wasn't with the boys; would they be unsettled staying in different houses, would they think I didn't care about them any more?

 We soon got to know the staff of our unwanted second home very well. The sister always looked as if she had just popped in on her way to an expensive night out, immaculately made up and calmness personified. The uniform gave the game away, but symbolised her attitude of unceasing care towards her patients. Her staff seemed to have imbibed her philosophy, to nursing if not to face-painting. I sometimes wondered if they cared about Heidi more than I did.

We had many visitors, who all seemed to find Heidi very loveable and interesting. One time I was sitting staring gloomily at the little figure in the cot, so thin and ill, looking at us with trusting eyes.

'She never smiles', I said.

'You'll have to smile at her first', our visitor replied. The point was well made. I didn't exactly feel like smiling, but I don't suppose Heidi did either.

Twenty miles away, yet big baby William had followed me. Sometimes during the long hours sitting with Heidi he would be there with us, mocking us with his sturdy limbs and healthy complexion. Jealousy and bitterness would wash over me as I fought to expel the image from my mind.

Just before Heidi had gone back into hospital I had written to a friend far away from the situation. I had shared my feelings about William and asked her to pray for me. The possibility of a real visit from him and his parents filled me with dread, but I knew I had to resolve my anger or there would always be a barrier between us and them.

Sure enough, before long they came to see us. At first I still did not want to look at William, but after a while God wonderfully changed my attitude. I was able to cuddle him and thank God for giving them a healthy first child. I suddenly saw how hard the situation must be for them, and remembered too that I had two healthy boys to be thankful for.

I phoned my faraway friend later to tell her we were now in hospital.

'How are you feeling now about William?' she asked.

I told her the story and discovered she had spent the day before praying and fasting for me. The rapid and striking answer was another brief glimpse of God in action, like a scrap of paper blown on a gale. I snatched the scrap from the wind and held it close. Whether near or far, our Christian brothers and sisters were with us in whatever ways they could be, and our Father was at work through them and in us. Though I still could not fathom or embrace the experience of deep pain he had led us into, I knew, somewhere deep within me, that he would lead us through it and out on the far side.

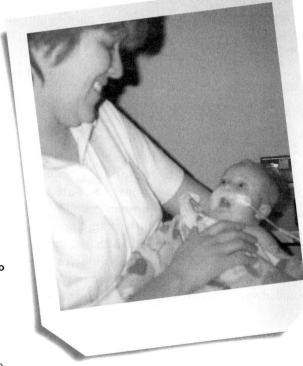

You'll have to smile at her first

A question of support

August 10th. 'She still isn't gaining any weight, despite the supplements she's on,' the heart consultant was saying soberly. She had been in for ten days now. 'Her heart is failing so badly that she's using up all that extra energy just keeping herself alive. Although it would be much safer if she were bigger, we will have to consider doing the operation soon now.'

August 13th. Further news which sent our emotions into hyperdrive and thoughts of the operation were shelved.

'The blood test showed up some abnormal cells. It's probably nothing to worry about. But there is a possibility of a problem with Heidi's bone marrow not producing blood cells as it should.'

'You mean leukaemia?' Liz's voice was quiet and colourless, but assaulted my eardrums as if it were a fierce scream. *Leukaemia! Nothing to worry about! Whatever else is going to happen to the poor child!*

'That is a possibility, but it is not unusual for the blood of very young babies with Down's syndrome to look like leukaemic blood. Leukaemia prevents cells from growing properly. So immature blood cells can look the same as leukaemic cells. But this is not a true leukaemia and quickly resolves itself when the blood fully develops.'

'But children with Down's are much more susceptible to leukaemia, aren't they.'

'Yes, that is true, but it is more likely to be just the blood picture giving that appearance. The symptom could be related to her heart condition. But I do need your consent to do a bone marrow test, which is the only way to know for sure'.

He left us, and once again we attempted vainly to comfort each other.

'Try to be calm', I said hopelessly. 'He said it will probably turn out to be nothing. There's no point worrying about something that is unlikely to happen.' Terribly logical, but I couldn't be rational myself, let alone expect Liz to be. And maybe he was just putting a positive gloss on it, to spare our feelings until it is confirmed. I kept that thought to myself, along with others that followed. I felt very sad for Heidi, but that demon was on my shoulder again... *Perhaps she will die from this...* I tried to shake it off, but couldn't, because it was not on my shoulder, it was inside my head, inside myself... *She's got so many problems, perhaps it would be better for her if she died...*

Better for her? Yes, it surely would be, but the terrible part was the thought that it would be better for me.

 A day's anxious wait; knowing the higher risk, leukaemia had been a fear in the back of my mind since Heidi had been born. Was this another foreboding that was about to become reality? There was nothing I could do, but my mind would not be clear of it, round and round it went like a manic goldfish.

August 14th. Finally the doctor came with the result.

'I'm delighted to tell you that Heidi's bone marrow result is normal', he smiled.

What a relief, it had been just a misleading blood picture. I needn't have wasted all that energy worrying about it.

One less anxiety, but there were still plenty of others. Of course, the worrying did nothing to ease Heidi's problems or mine. **'Do not be anxious about anything...'** How I wished I could obey the Biblical writer's instruction, but it seemed impossible. *Oh God, help me to leave my worries with you.*

August 16th. By now I felt the stretching tension was coming close to breaking point. Heidi was finally beginning to gain a little weight, so her operation had been postponed to see if this continued. There was no immediate prospect of her coming home and I felt I must be with the boys more, so we moved back home. Each day I drove to the hospital, but it felt a little more like being a family again.

For two weeks Heidi continued to gain weight, painfully slowly and sometimes with depressing downward blips, but the trend was definitely in the right direction. The doctors began to discuss the possibility of her coming home, but this would mean learning to put her naso-gastric feeding tube down. She frequently grabbed it and pulled it out, so it would be impractical to take her to hospital every time it needed doing. I am naturally squeamish and felt very nervous about the responsibility; would I be able to do it properly?

I shared my concern with a nurse friend from church, who immediately offered to come over and learn with me. It was a great support having her alongside to help, and the thought that someone would be reasonably close if I got stuck at home was very comforting. Despite my misgivings I soon got the hang of it, together with the technical side of the procedure; operating, priming and correcting failures of the electrical pump. My teacher pronounced me competent and I gave thanks for another answered prayer. Now I would have to do it for real, at home alone.

August was almost gone when Heidi came home, bringing further challenges. Her overnight feed was automatic, when it didn't wake me up bleeping insistently in the small hours like a non tube-fed baby. During the day she was tube-fed manually every two or three hours, with an energy-rich concoction I had to make up. Each feed was a laborious palaver taking up to half an hour to complete. And the completion didn't last long as most of it would reappear shortly afterwards. This made the whole procedure rather unsatisfying for me as well as Heidi. There was also an impressive selection of vital medicines to remember to administer at regular intervals. For my spare moments there was a list of exercises Kate the physio had left before Heidi had gone into hospital. I also wanted to give the boys the time I had been unable to share with them while Heidi had been in hospital.

'Do not be anxious about anything, but in everything by prayer and petition, with thanksgiving, present your requests to God.' (Philippians 4:6)

The verse was never far away. Though I was still struggling with the first part, the 'everything' was becoming more of a reality. I was cultivating an attitude of prayer about each little problem of the day, albeit only because my circumstances were forcing me to do so. Drained of my own resources, I knew the truth of God's strength being made perfect in my weakness as I prayed my way through the next feed or nappy change.

Sunday September 3rd, the first opportunity for Heidi to have her official welcome into our church family. This is one of Pastor Paul's favourite duties and usually happens the first time a baby is brought to church, more commonly at about two weeks old rather than two months. This time there was not, for us at least, the usual feeling of joyful thanksgiving as we walked to the front of the church and handed the tiny bundle over to him. But as he cradled Heidi in his arms the sense of a shared sorrow and commitment was almost tangible. Liz and I, Daniel and Tim sat in front of Paul, love cascading over us from the rows behind as he spoke.

'Today is a very special day in the life of this church and Heidi is a very special person. She's special to us all because she has special needs. I'm sure she's going to be a blessing to you as a family and to us as a church. We feel a sense of privilege because God has given her to us as well, to love and to care for and to pray for. Heidi is going to need some special support and I'm sure we take it into our hearts today to care for this little girl as long as her life is spared.

'When Heidi was born I was preaching each week from the book of Malachi. I knew this verse was coming up and it kept going round in my mind as I thought of Heidi:

'They shall be mine,' says the LORD of hosts, 'on the day that I make them my jewels.' (Malachi 3:17)

'It is our prayer that Heidi will be the Lord's, and that one day she will be a jewel in the crown of our Lord Jesus Christ.'

These were no mere easy words, but a sincere promise of commitment from the church to Heidi. We knew then, and time has proved, that this support would not fade away after a few weeks or months. It would be a rock in a storm-driven sea, because it was not manufactured. It was the natural overflow of a love for Jesus, the one whose actions demonstrated such deep care for the weak, the disabled, the disadvantaged people of the world.

The Importance of Being

 'I'm sure she's going to be a blessing to you as a family and to us as a church'.

We had been unable then to share Paul's confidence, but time has proved the truth of his words.

Some people prefer to use the politically correct term 'differently abled'. This seems absurd to me; being, for example, unable to walk is not an alternative ability. Perhaps there is a feeling that 'disabled' equates with 'devalued'. This is a sad reflection on our sinful human nature which tends to rate people on what they look like or what they can do.

Yes, there is no doubt that Heidi is disabled. Yet there is a sense in which the ugly phrase 'differently abled' is true of her. She has talents which are especially hers within our family, whether they are connected with her Down's syndrome or not.

'Are you all right my dear brother?' Heidi's head was cocked to one side, face full of tender concern and an arm affectionately resting on Tim's shoulder. The contortions of his face began to soften, the seething breaths quietened and the clenched fists unwound. He flung his opened hands around his sister and held her tight.

We had been unable to communicate across the wall of anger, but our tiny four year old had scaled it effortlessly. Despite himself, Tim was unable to resist her. Someone else could have used the same words, expressed the same love, but an intangible ingredient would have been missing from the recipe. This was not a unique occurrence; Tim was going through a difficult period of struggling with uncontrollable anger. By no means always, but often Heidi could communicate with him when no-one else could, and the rage would evaporate as quickly as it had come.

One day we had a visitor who had no hands, but in their place metal claws. Out came Heidi to see what interesting person had just arrived. *Oh no, she's going to scream and run away, or at least make some inappropriate remark…it's at moments like this I'm glad her speech isn't always very clear…*

Heidi bounced up to him, grinning broadly. She took both claws in her hands by way of greeting, as naturally as if most of her friends had this new style of hand.

Before she started school Heidi loved to go to a drop-in centre the church runs on a Tuesday morning. Some of the regulars were lonely, some struggled with a drink problem, some felt rejected by society. To Heidi they were just friends and she loved being the centre of attention as she showed off and pestered them to read books to her. If she spotted any of them at church on Sunday she would give them a great greeting.

'Hello George', she enthused after one service, and then, thinking quickly, presented him with her just-produced work of art. 'I drawed this picture for you.' George was delighted and the two of them chatted away happily for the next few minutes.

 One Sunday two refugees from Sierra Leone came to church for the first time. She greeted each in turn, putting one hand on his knee and pressing the other into his palm.

'Hello, what's your name?' she asked, face alight with obviously genuine delight to see them. Yes, adults had made them welcome, but they were clearly touched

by this little girl. Fleeing war, leaving friends and family, just arrived in a strange country so far away, she had made them feel at home. One of them, Augustine, she often prayed for, although she insisted on referring to him as 'Poor Gustin'.

Prejudice: something many people struggle against in different ways and to varying degrees, and the root of so much suffering throughout the world. We may rail against it from our comfortable vantage point atop the moral high ground, only to find it lurking within ourselves in another form. Even the acceptable face of politically correct society is deeply culpable; although such people would be mortified at the suggestion. It is a strangely warped ethos which with one face champions equal opportunities for disabled people and with the other promotes their destruction before they are born. This

must do wonders for the self esteem of those who survive the cull.

Heidi has no concept of prejudice, although she is sometimes a victim of it. She simply accepts and appreciates people for who they are. Having her around has shown me more clearly the tendency within myself to judge people by the cover or stick a convenient label on them. Whether disabled or disturbed, black or white, militant atheist or Moslem fundamentalist, fragrant beauty or odoursome vagrant, sparkling company or duller than a beige tea cosy; I want to see people as God does— all his creations and of great worth.

'Jake is my boyfriend', Heidi announced proudly.

'Oo er', teased Daniel.

'Are you going to marry him?' Tim asked.

Just children playing an age old game, yet I feel a sudden pang of sadness. From time to time some little thing chimes a reminder of Heidi's limitations. In all probability she never will get married, or go to university, or whatever it might be.

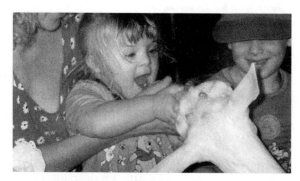

Every day crammed with fun

Then a raucous laugh interrupts my reverie and I see her, head thrown back as she revels in some hilarious joke. My knitted brows ease into a smile. It is impossible to be sad for long with Heidi around. How can you feel sorry for someone who has such a great time?

'Quality of life'. A well-worn phrase these days, usually used negatively. A phrase often used to justify curtailing the life of an unborn someone with a disability. Perhaps someone like Heidi. It is also sometimes used to describe children or adults:

'Poor things, they have no quality of life'. How patronising and presumptuous!

Think of an 'average', 'normal' person. He works in a factory. Doesn't enjoy it much, but it pays the bills—just. As long as the factory stays open. Those maintenance payments really eat into his wages. Why did he have that stupid fling which wrecked his marriage? Hardly ever sees the kids now. Nights out drinking dull the pain and loneliness a bit, but he can't afford them too often.

Then think of Heidi. Perfectly content with her lot; every day crammed with fun, not a care in the world. Who has the better quality of life?

Surely disability is a very poor yardstick to use. Happiness, contentment, peace; these are better measures, and Heidi exhibits them to a large degree.

In an ultimate sense they are to be found in a personal relationship with Jesus Christ, who is the only way to the fullest quality of life.

Catch–22

Despite all the difficulties, this couple of weeks at home was to prove a haven of respite; an eye in the midst of the tornado that was about to grab us once again and hurl us around with strengthend force.

Suddenly Heidi picked up a nasty cough; then her complexion turned gradually bluer, her breathing became laboured and her chest was recessing badly. All the bad old signs were back. I took her to the doctor who sent me straight to hospital. Yes, she was in heart failure again and now she had pneumonia too. Once again she was lying helplessly in a hospital cot, tubes everywhere, a plastic box over her face supplying oxygen.

I was summoned to the doctor's office to discuss some blood test results. His face was grave as I entered.

'I'm afraid I have more bad news for you. The tests suggest Heidi may have leukaemia'.

'Oh, that's nothing', I replied. 'Her blood showed a leukaemic picture at Birmingham, but they did a marrow and it was fine'.

'I'd still like her to have the bone marrow again. It's probably best for her to have it at Birmingham.'

When I got back to the ward there was a nurse from a cancer charity waiting to talk to me about coping with leukaemia. They're still taking this pretty seriously, I thought. I wasn't worried, so I sent her away. I told her they had got it wrong; I was sure it was still just the blood picture. But as I travelled in the ambulance to Birmingham that evening I was pleased we were going there, as I was confident she would receive the best treatment for the heart failure and pneumonia.

Friday September 15. Big bad days were starting to come thick and fast now. The leukaemia consultant came round with Heidi's results.

'It's bad news, I'm afraid. It's clear from the blood test alone that Heidi has leukaemia. I don't need the bone marrow result to confirm it.'

At first we struggled to accept it; after the previous experience we tried to believe this was the same again. But the truth was irresistible; this was no picture, a mere two dimensional representation of reality. It was a genuine megakaryoblastic leukaemia, cancer of the blood, with all the dreadful repercussions those chilling words evoke.

'She hasn't got much strength to cope with chemotherapy because of her heart condition,' the consultant was saying. 'That is why she was susceptible to pneumonia, which has weakened her further. She needs her heart operation to enable her to gain strength, but she can't have it because of the leukaemia. I'm afraid she is likely to fade away very quickly.' This was some Catch–22, but it was no work of fiction.

'We can try chemotherapy if you would like us to, although it is a very invasive treatment and would be painful for Heidi.'

'Is there any chance of success?'

'A slim chance. If the initial treatment were successful there would be quite a high chance of the leukaemia coming back within the next couple of years. The incidence of recurrence is much higher in children with Down's syndrome. Talk it through over the weekend; perhaps you could let us know your decision on Monday'.

Once our numbed heads began to function again they moved swiftly into high speed mode as we discussed and turned over incessantly in our minds this momentous decision.

If there is even a remote chance, perhaps we ought to go ahead; do we have the right to deny Heidi that possibility...but do we have the right to put her poor suffering body through any more pain...hasn't she suffered enough? Even if she came through, and recovered from pneumonia, she would still have a huge heart operation to face...am I thinking like this for Heidi's sake, or because it would be the easier way out for me? I want us to make the right decision, not one that I've persuaded myself is best for Heidi because of some subconscious agenda of my own. Oh God, make the right way clear to us.

'Commit your works to the Lord and your thoughts will be established.' (Proverbs 16:3) The truth of the proverb had been proved in our lives many times. We prayed that our zig-zagging thoughts would be settled by Monday.

'A time to be born and a time to die'…are we taking God's place if we don't go ahead? Are we trying to make his decision for him? Or perhaps he has made his decision; he is trying to tell us that it is time for his own special possession, his jewel, to become part of his crown. His heart is full of perfect love for Heidi, he doesn't see her Down's syndrome, her failing heart, her near-useless body. He loves her unconditionally. Does he really want us to prolong her suffering, indeed exacerbate it, probably for no purpose? What if she came through everything and then it came back in eighteen months time? We'd be so much more attached to her. She'd have to go through it all again, then probably die…that would be so much worse. But should that fear come into our decision now?

The first sermon I'd heard after Heidi had been born had contained a wonderful description of heaven; no pain, no sadness, only perfect joy. I'd thought of Heidi then and it came back to me now. A powerful, very literal, image came into my mind of Heidi safe in God's strong arms. *Nobody will be sticking needles into you there, Heidi.* I felt a peaceful certainty that if God wanted to take her, that is where she would be. Yet there was also a terrible fear of losing her. As I felt this I realised how much I was beginning to love and accept her. Yes, she would be safe in God's arms; but I wanted her in **my** arms.

Cliffhanger

Saturday September 16.

'You know Heidi is very poorly, don't you Daniel.'

'Yes mummy. Will she be poorly for much longer?'

We had tried several times gently to prepare Daniel for the possibility of Heidi dying. He was old enough to be deeply shocked if his much-loved baby sister never came home. We wanted to cushion this potential blow, but had so far been unable to communicate the message. Now that the possibility seemed inevitable we had to try once more.

'You know Daniel, sometimes when people are very poorly, they die, don't they.'

'Yes mummy, I know.'

'Sometimes God takes little children to heaven, Daniel. Sometimes even babies.'

'Yes mummy'.

'God might want to take Heidi to be with him, Daniel. It would be very sad for us, but she would be very happy there, wouldn't she. She wouldn't be weak and poorly any more.'

'God will make her better.'

Once again, that was the end of the conversation as far as Daniel was concerned. The simple faith of a three year old was stronger than ours; he had prayed for this and he was sure God would answer. But today could be Daniel's and Tim's last chance to see their little sister. Although it would be another emotion-shredding experience, we had to take them to say goodbye.

'No, this way boys! Follow the green line.'

'Don't run off! Come back! You'll get lost, or crash into a trolley!'

We were somewhat surprised to find we had all made it to the door of Heidi's ward.

'Now boys, calm down. Remember the children in here are very poorly.

Heidi might look different from last time you saw her. She'll have more tubes and things and she might look more unwell. But she's still the same Heidi, isn't she.'

The boys, of course, were desperate to skip the lecture and get straight in.

'Hello Heidi!'

'Can I hold her?'

Excited faces, shining eyes. Throats swelled, eyes brimmed as we watched. They couldn't have cared less about all the drips and monitors. Of course she was still the same Heidi, still their precious little sister. But for us the black cloud came down even lower, threatening to envelop us in its oppressive power. *This decision is too big for us to deal with. What shall we do?*

Some decisions about Heidi had been simple to make, even if not easy. On that terrible first day, we had both known we would keep her; there had been no need for discussion. For us it was clear cut, although for many others in that situation it is not. But if anyone thinks this decision that was pressing down on us should have been one of those black and white scenarios, they could not be further off target.

You'd say you uphold the Christian belief in the utmost sanctity of life…but now, when theory hits reality, are you chucking it in? Does belief in the sanctity of life mean preserving it at any cost? Is it necessarily valuing a person most highly to sustain their life by technology when their whole body is screaming 'I give up'? I don't know the answer. Perhaps it is sometimes yes and sometimes no. I do know that this situation is very, very grey. WHAT SHALL WE DO?

Before long, being little boys, they had had enough. After some gentle persuasion to give Heidi more than the briefest goodbye, they were off, rushing ahead, whooping with glee, full of life and free of care. We followed, full of care, our minds left behind with the still, quiet little girl whose life had almost ebbed right away.

We shared our situation with Pastor Paul and his wife Hazel and another wise couple. Both separately struggled through the dilemma with us. Eventually both conversations came to the same conclusion and the decision became clearer. We would proceed with chemotherapy for the moment, but would stop if we felt the prognosis had become hopeless. We felt at peace for Heidi, with ourselves and before God about the decision we had made.

Sunday September 17. It was a welcome relief to be invited out to dinner and tea. At teatime Liz suddenly felt she must phone the hospital to check how Heidi was.

'I'm so glad you phoned; we've been trying to contact you all day. Heidi is much worse; can you come straight over?'

We rushed to Birmingham. Now we were ready to give them our decision on chemotherapy, was it was being taken out of our hands?

The tension grew by the second as we ran along the familiar tortuous route through the rambling old hospital. What would we find? Sudden relief washed over us; there she was in her familiar place, calm and quiet, looking as if she was wondering what all the fuss was about. But her medical notes revealed the truth hidden beneath the current veneer of calm. Just two hours before she had suddenly become feverish, temperature 40, pulse 200, pneumonia worse. Her heart consultant had come in to deal with it, although it was his weekend off. Now he wanted to speak to us.

'She has come through this for now, but it was touch and go. At one point we thought she would have to go into Intensive Care to be ventilated. She improved just in time, but it is quite likely this will happen again. With all her other problems, her body is too weak to fight the pneumonia. The doctor in Intensive Care doesn't feel she should go there and I must say I agree. I'm afraid it would really be a hopeless situation, just putting her through more suffering. We certainly can't consider chemotherapy unless her condition improves.'

It seemed even more inevitable now. When they had left us the stress and emotion took over and I wept on Liz's shoulder. It was the first time that I knew I really loved Heidi; just as I was about to lose her.

Monday September 18. Through the night Heidi had managed to maintain her tenuous grip on the knife-edged ridge she was crawling along. Several times she had scrabbled for handholds as her temperature, blood pressure, heart rate and breathing had fluctuated, but by morning the sheer drops on either side had become a little less threatening. Her head was still under an oxygen box, but she was more stable and peaceful.

Today's shock was good news, which made a refreshing change.

'There are fewer leukaemic cells in Heidi's blood today. It is most unusual. It may just be a blip, but we'll monitor it over the next few days before we go ahead with any treatment. I suggest we review the situation on Friday.'

We held our breath through Tuesday, Wednesday, Thursday, hardly daring to believe it as Heidi remained fairly stable and the number of leukaemic cells steadily waned.

They think it's all over

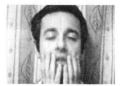
Friday September 22.

Review day—and no leukaemic cells left at all! The specialist could not understand it; he had never seen it happen before. As far as we know he had no Christian faith, but he described it to us as a miracle. Although many people had been praying for this very thing, although we have an unchanging God of miracles; yet it was hard to believe it ourselves.

Thank you Lord. You really can still do the impossible. Yes, I always believed it was true, but when I see it before my own eyes, in my own daughter, it really blows my mind. Forgive me for all my anger and doubting…

It's an incredibly weird feeling, but it's hard to adjust to thinking that she might live now. I'd just become used to thinking in terms of her death being inevitable. Although perhaps the leukaemia will come back again next week. Or next year. But God has healed her. Does that mean she won't get it again? That would be just an interesting theological question if it wasn't my child lying there. Stop it, we mustn't get entangled in worries about leukaemia. We've got to think about the future again now. The future, with Heidi. How will we cope?

We had a couple of hours to contemplate the future. Then another high-velocity ball was fired into the crazy pinball machine inside our heads. In the afternoon Heidi suddenly became worse. Her skin temperature fell so low she had to be warmed up in an incubator. She was examined and found to be in kidney failure. No more leukaemia, but now another life-threatening condition. *Oh God, what are you doing?*

Yet again her condition was stabilised, and it was time for another deja-vu conference with the doctors. This time the Intensive Care anaesthetist was there too.

'Her condition may well deteriorate again due to the kidney failure, to the extent that she would need to go on a ventilator in the Intensive Care Unit (ICU). Now that the leukaemia situation has changed I would be happy to take her in, as the prognosis would not be completely hopeless. But you may not wish to put her through it in view of her overall condition. The necessary care would be unpleasant for her. It would be painful for you too to see her attached to so many machines, drips, electrodes, especially if it is the end of her life. You may prefer us not to resuscitate her if she is that ill. But we are very happy to do whatever you want. Have a look around the ICU so you know what it is like and let us know later.'

Another huge decision, not much time. We forced our emotionally exhausted minds to concentrate as we walked around the ICU. So soon after the good news on the leukaemia. Every time she seemed to improve a little, another thudding blow came in. It seemed impossible that she could recover, she just had too many problems. The ICU itself didn't feel too bad. Yes, there were more machines and monitors, but the staff seemed just as caring and attentive. *Should we put her through any more? Hasn't she suffered enough? But if there's a chance, we can't deny it to her …*

'Have you decided what you would like us to do about ICU?'

The doctor came before we had finally decided. After speaking with us for a while, he discerned our underlying feelings:

'We'll take her into ICU and resuscitate her if we need to.'

Saturday September 23. Heidi was more settled again today, the kidney failure seemingly under control. We left her sleeping peacefully and went home to find the boys.

Sunday September 24.

The subject of the sermon in church this morning demonstrated once again God's perfect timing:

'Fear not for I have redeemed you; I have called you by name; you are mine. When you pass through the waters, I will be with you; and when you pass through the rivers, they will not sweep over you. When you walk through the fire, you will not be burned.' (Isaiah 43:1,2)

After the previous Sunday's experience we had brought a mobile phone with us. Immediately after the service its foreboding ring thrust us back into the furnace. The hospital wanted us to come straight over again.

Heidi's kidney failure was much worse. It seemed very likely that she would need to go into Intensive Care.

Peace is a very familiar term, but the common concept of it is a limited one. Most of the entrants in a painting competition on the subject had this two-dimensional perspective. Their submissions depicted idyllic scenes; gentle streams bubbling through tranquil meadows; motionless trees etched against a backcloth of pure azure skies. But the winning entry was shocking in its violence; towering seas crashing against the cliffs, foam whipped by the vicious wind. Many who viewed the exhibits were baffled; what had this to do with peace? But the careful observer was rewarded by the sight of a tiny bird sheltering in a niche in the cliff, perfectly still.

It is easy to have some peace when things are going well. However, as we drove to the hospital that day we experienced that incredible, deepest peace which is superimposed in sharp-edged relief upon a life in turmoil. It is the peace of God, and truly surpasses all understanding. We had just received a letter from my dad which contained this line:

'We cannot tell what God has in store for many lives from the deep waters you are now so especially passing through.' Indeed we were in deep waters, but at that moment we knew God was in total control and was working for the good of us and others, whatever the outcome. We knew he was with us, and with Heidi, as we sang our way along the motorway:

> Be still, my soul; the Lord is on your side;
> bear patiently the weight of grief or pain;
> leave to your God to order and provide;
> through every change he faithful will remain.
> Be still, my soul; your gracious, heavenly Friend
> through thorny ways leads to a joyful end.

> Be still, my soul; your God will undertake
> to guide the future as he has the past.
> Your hope, your confidence, let nothing shake;
> all now mysterious shall be bright at last.
> Be still, my soul; the waves and winds still know
> the voice of Christ that ruled them here below.

Be still, my soul; the day is hastening on
when we shall be forever with the Lord,
when disappointment, grief and fear are gone,
sorrow forgotten, love's pure joys restored.
Be still, my soul; when change and tears are past,
in his safe presence we shall meet at last.   (PRAISE! HYMN BOOK VERSION)

 I'd like to have that one at her funeral ... what an awful thought, we don't even know if she's died yet ... I won't mention it to Steve. Quick, I'll start singing another one ...

God holds the key of all unknown
And I am glad;
If other hands should hold the key,
Or if he trusted it to me,
I might be sad.

I expect lots of people will come to her funeral...I saw the tiny coffin being carried down the aisle, imagined us watching, failing to dam the tears...we could have that hymn about God's jewels... 'Like the stars of the morning, his bright crown adorning, they shall shine in their beauty, bright gems for his crown'...oh no, I shouldn't be thinking like this, she might still be alive...I won't say anything to Liz.

I was so far away I got stuck in the wrong lane past some roadworks and couldn't leave at the right junction.

Why did I have to do that today of all days ... it will probably take another half an hour now ... we might miss her ...

On other days this would have had me climbing the wall, but today the peace kept reigning.

Running along the covered walkway, bursting through the door onto the ward; what would we find? Would her familiar cot be ominously empty, Heidi in Intensive Care ... or worse? But no, there she was, lying peacefully;

back from the brink again. The roller coaster had emerged from the latest blind bend. How many more sickening twists would we be flung violently round? But we didn't want the journey to end, because it seemed that the end would be even worse than the ride.

 Wednesday September 27. No more alarms since Sunday and the kidney problem had improved greatly. Steve was out working and I was at home looking after a poorly Daniel and trying to catch up with the hundred and one jobs that had been left undone. Despite the ongoing support from my faithful band of helpers, there were some things that only I could do.

I phoned the hospital at about 11 am for the latest update.

'Heidi is much brighter today, she's alert and looking around. Hopefully she might be able to have her heart operation soon'.

I said we would be over the next day to discuss this and put the phone down feeling much more positive. If Heidi could get through that operation she would be so much better equipped to cope with other infections. Maybe that would really be a corner turned.

But before long the ward sister was on the telephone again. At about 2 o'clock Heidi had suddenly turned blue and stopped breathing. The crash team had managed to resuscitate her and she was about to be moved to Intensive Care for further treatment. I called a friend who immediately dropped everything to come and look after the boys. I rushed to the hospital, alone. This time there had been no reprieve from Intensive Care. She was only alive because she was on a ventilator, forcing her to breathe because her straining lungs had given up. It hadn't seemed too bad when we had been round the ICU the other day, but I couldn't bear the sight of my own daughter surrounded with so much machinery, just a cog in the middle of an artificial life form. It was too much like the final waiting room. I went out and longed for Steve's arrival.

This event decided the doctors that Heidi could wait no longer for her heart operation; it was now or never. Although she was terribly weak, making the operation very risky, her condition would never improve with her heart failing so badly. It was scheduled for the following day, subject to a final blood test to check that the leukaemia had not returned.

One of the crash team doctors came round and described the moment Heidi had responded to their efforts at resuscitation that afternoon:

'There we were, frantically working away, trying to get her breathing going again as she lay there, unmoving. Suddenly she opened her eyes, looked up at us and grinned from ear to ear, as if to say 'Hello, it's very nice to see you all, giving me so much attention!''

As we waited for the long hours to tick away we wondered if we would ever see her smile again.

Carry on, Doctor

 That moment turned out to be one of the first glimpses of the character Heidi would become. Maybe her early months enabled her to 'bond' with doctors in general, because she has loved them ever since. This is a good thing, because she sees plenty of them and it would make life very difficult if she didn't want to go. As well as heart check-ups and blood tests, she has had regular tests of eyes and ears and complete medicals due to having Down's syndrome. She has also had many unscheduled visits for sundry minor ailments exacerbated by her heart and chest weakness. Not to mention her visits to a paediatrician regarding an ongoing constipation problem. She is always most indignant if another member of the family goes to the doctor without her,

and even the dreaded injections have failed to dim her enthusiasm for medical people.

'I'm going to the doctor's to see the nurse', she announced excitedly to everyone she met that morning. You wouldn't be so chirpy if you knew what you were in for, I thought grimly. My stomach was beginning to knot at the prospect. I was taking two of them to do a job lot, so it would be double trouble for me.

The waiting room was crowded and we had to squeeze into a narrow gap on the seat. The man next to us didn't see any need to move up, but Heidi soon found a solution.

'Here you are man, read this'. She picked up the magazine that sat between us and him, plonked it down on his lap and planted herself in the space thus liberated. Thankfully he was amused and after a few minutes we noticed he had obeyed her instruction and was absorbed in an article.

When the dreaded moment came Heidi greeted the nurse with great enthusiasm, took her hand and went into the surgery like a lamb to the slaughter. She watched in open-mouthed amazement and growing disapproval while her sibling kicked and yelled as the sleeve was yanked up; then screamed without drawing breath for two minutes after the event. When it was finally her turn, Heidi held out her arm keenly and grinned at the nurse.

'Oh don't', the nurse groaned. 'I always feel guilty doing this and you're making it even worse'.

I shut my eyes and prepared for the howl as the needle pierced her skin, but she just flinched slightly and didn't make a sound. Maybe after everything she has been through it didn't seem a big deal.

'Goodbye nurse, see you soon', chirped Heidi, grin still at the ready. 'Thank you for giving me my 'jection.'

Soon after Heidi started school she had to make one of her visits to the paediatrician about her constipation. This time there was a young man with the doctor.

'Would you mind if I used Heidi to show my student some features of Down's syndrome?' she asked. I replied that it was fine.

'The first thing to notice is this', the paediatrician said, pointing to the badge on Heidi's school jumper. 'Many children with Down's syndrome now go to a mainstream school and integrate very well.'

Heidi delightedly showed off hands, face, chest, limbs and so on, pleased as ever to be the centre of attention.

'Well done Heidi, you're a star', said the doctor when she had finished.

'I'm not a star', retorted Heidi indignantly. 'I'm a superstar!'

On the next visit a junior doctor was present.

'Hello lady', said Heidi cheerfully to the paediatrician, and, turning to her colleague, 'Hello doctor'.

'The lady's a doctor too, Heidi,' I quickly chipped in.

'No she's not, she's a lady', returned Heidi emphatically. I knew that trying to persuade her otherwise would be futile.

'It's because you haven't got a stethoscope', I explained apologetically.

When she had been examined Heidi turned to the junior while the paediatrician discussed Heidi's condition with me.

'Can you read these books to me?' she asked, with irresistible pleading eyes.

Finally we were ready to go.

'Say goodbye, Heidi'.

'Goodbye, doctor. Thank you for reading books to me. Goodbye lady.' Then, not wishing to be impolite, 'Thank you for..er..thank you for..er..' Suddenly inspiration struck, with a big grin: 'Thank you for lookin' at my bottom!'

Our GP's are all very interested in and fond of Heidi. After one cheerful, chatty encounter, the doctor said

'You know, with all her limitations, I'm sure Heidi is more like God meant us to be than most of us are'.

Back to the future

Thursday September 28. The blood test was clear; the operation was on. Steve's parents and mine came up and sat with me through the interminable hours Heidi was in theatre. Steve had to work and would arrive later. He'd said with typical male logic that he couldn't do anything while they were operating anyway, but I still wished he was there. Eventually he arrived and after further waiting the surgeon came out.

'The operation was successful and Heidi has been stable since she has come back to ICU. It was more complicated than we were expecting. We haven't been able to seal completely the leak in one valve, but there is only minor leakage now. She will need another operation on this when she is two or three. She's not out of danger yet, but she's a real fighter. I'm confident she'll pull through.'

As we rejoiced and thanked God we saw what so easily could have been us. A young couple, distraught, vacant, disbelieving. Their news had been so different. No doubt they too had been to some extent prepared for it, yet the finality of death was still deeply shocking. Our hearts went out to them. We could so easily empathise with their feelings of empty despair from which we had been so narrowly spared.

Over the following days Heidi slowly but surely gained strength. As expected, she was in ICU for longer than the usual time. This was due to her extreme weakness when she had the operation. However on October 5 she returned to the children's ward and after a further ten days she was well enough to come home.

While she had been in hospital there had always been the thought that she might relapse again. After so many such experiences it was hard to come away from that mindset. Psychologically the move home again seemed to be the last hurdle. We started to allow ourselves to believe that she really would survive.

Yes, I've got to love and accept her fully now. I've not had to think in those terms recently, but she's with us for keeps...or at least for the moment. That placard inscribed 'LEUKAEMIA' in big black letters was up in the back of my mind again, as it has been periodically to this day. *After all we've been through it shouldn't be a difficulty to accept her. God has given me my daughter back from the dead! Oh Lord, I am so thankful, I really am. If you had not been guiding our decisions, we wouldn't have her now. If we'd given her up when it seemed so hopeless; if we'd said no to resuscitation in ICU... It doesn't bear thinking about. I do love her, but she's still got Down's syndrome, she still needs tube feeding, she's still going to be so demanding. Oh Lord, help me to cope. Help me to accept her. Help me to value her as much as I value the boys.*

Stares in their eyes

Just one week of having Heidi at home and it would be half term. In the distant past we had entertained hopes of going away for the week with three other families we knew. After a couple of days of coping with Heidi a thought wandered aimlessly into my head. *Perhaps we could go after all...we've missed out on our summer holiday...it would be wonderful to get away after all this...no don't be stupid, we couldn't possibly take her away so soon.* I tried to banish the thought from my mind, but it was too persistent to ignore. There would be two nurses in the group after all, as well as several young girls who would be delighted to help with the tube feeding, nappy changing and so on. We asked her doctors, who saw no problem.

So the following Monday saw us setting off for Wales in the small hours. Heidi's night time continuous tube feeding contraption was stuck in place above her seat. It felt great to be going on holiday, until we stopped for breakfast at a Bad Cook, or whatever those places are called. Steve got Heidi out of the car, but forgot about her inseparable companion, the milk machine. I crouched in the freezing cold car park for the next ten minutes, threading the tube back down Heidi's

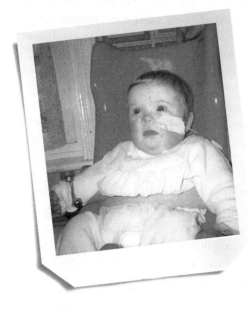

Everyone in the cafe swivelled towards Heidi, their eyes stuck out on stalks as they gawped in tasteless fascination.

throat, reattaching the tube to her face (two layers of different sticky tapes to avoid damaging her skin) and repriming the pump so it didn't turn itself off. So we were feeling rather less relaxed by the time we finally made it inside. Inside was ten times worse, because as we stepped through the door a sudden deathly hush descended. Servers stopped serving in mid-splat and waitresses stood stock still, although that was hardly noticeable. Everyone in the cafe swivelled towards Heidi, their eyes stuck out on stalks as they gawped in tasteless fascination. No, of course I was not in the least oversensitive, neither am I exaggerating at all. As we clattered our way towards the partial relief of a table, anger and hurt welled with the tears. I felt like screaming at them, 'Yes, she's got Down's syndrome! And sticky tape on her face! Have a good stare, why don't you!'

I sank into a seat and buried my head. *Whatever had made me think it was a good idea to go away? This is going to be a nightmare, people staring at her all week. It's not fair! Why does she have to have Down's syndrome? Why can't she be a lovely normal baby, with people cooing over her? Why does she have to have this horrible ugly pump and tube? I want to go home and shut myself away…*

'BLEEP! BLEEP! BLEEP!' *That stupid pump! What's gone wrong now?* The eyes all swung smartly round to attention. *I hope they rick their necks,* I thought, as I took the stage once more to remove the airlock which had triggered Act Two. *Let them stare. I'll show them I can sort this out calmly and efficiently.*

Things could only get better, and thankfully did. There were lots of things for the children to do at the caravan park where we were staying, and they loved playing together. I still noticed people staring at Heidi, or else quickly looking the other way. They couldn't win, really. Steve said it was just human nature, they weren't meaning to be rude. I tried to ignore it and managed to cope, most of the time.

We came across another little girl with Down's in the soft play area. She was about a year old, crawling around and having great fun. Her older brother and sister were playing with her and clearly adored her. We chatted to her parents who were very happy and positive about her. It made me feel a little better myself, until Steve pointed out an older girl who also had Down's. She had what I thought of as a stereotypical Down's haircut and glasses. What a hypocrite I was, putting her in a box straightaway. She was about ten, but playing at a far younger level. The negativity came flooding back; I wanted Heidi to be capable and attractive, not left behind and labelled. I was going to do everything within my power to help her achieve what I wanted, but would she ever reach my aspirations? I wanted to stop watching the girl who was unwittingly saddening me, but I couldn't. My eyes were magnetised; although, of course, I didn't stare.

Five years on and it's still a struggle sometimes. One day I came back fed up and exhausted after a marathon session at Safeway's.

'Stare, stare, stare!', I let off at Steve. 'Why do people have to do it? Haven't they seen anyone with Down's syndrome before?'

'They were probably staring at you', Steve replied nonchalantly without interrupting his gaze at the newspaper. The remaining steam dissipated rapidly as I preened myself.

'Thank you darling', I simpered.

'No, I meant they were probably thinking "Why ever is that barmy woman dragging four little kids round a supermarket?"'

He's so unobservant he never notices anyone staring in any case. Typical insensitive man.

We made our way contentedly homewards after the holiday. The unwelcome break on the outward journey was thankfully a fading memory. But we were soon reminded that such incidents were never far away. A rendezvous en route for fish and chips with the other families had seemed like a good idea. As we struggled back to the car afterwards with three tired children, it seemed less of a good idea. While reinstalling Heidi in the car her tube became dislodged. And the pump got airlocked. Then I dropped a vital piece of the mechanism on the ground. Naturally, the car was parked on a hill, so the bit rolled away. It was a dark night. My slowly-recharged patience level was plummeting, while the stress gauge shot back up. Eventually we got underway again, thinking enviously of our friends, halfway home by now. Mental note: next time take sandwiches.

A passage to Africa

 By the next morning we had recovered from the journey and felt the time away had done us good. Hopefully we would have a stable period now to get used to having Heidi around and rebuild our family equilibrium.

Later that day Heidi developed a bad cough. Her breathing became laboured, her complexion deteriorated and the following day she was once more in hospital with pneumonia. For a while it was touch and go again; had she been given back to us just to be taken away? But this time the antibiotics were able to take effect. Now that her heart was working properly her still-tiny body had enough strength to fight the infection. For a long time her lungs were still a weakness so that any infection rapidly became pneumonia. Nevertheless she made it through the winter with only two more short stays in hospital.

There was still a great deal more to do for Heidi than a normal healthy baby. She was still being tube fed by the wretched unreliable pump overnight and the even more detested manual method by day. There were lots of appointments with teacher, physiotherapist, dietician, speech therapist, health visitor, hearing specialist and sundry doctors. These were often helpful, but all took time and usually left me with a 'homework sheet' of exercises or targets to pursue with Heidi. After all the months of stress, we were exhausted and felt in severe need of a real holiday, on our own, away from everything. The alluring prospect of exchanging a cold, wet English January for sun, sea and sand had to be worth some thought, although it seemed impossibly impractical.

Peter and Janet (among others) did say we must tell them if there was anything they could do to help...I know they meant it, so I wouldn't be afraid to ask...I mean get Steve to ask...Janet is a doctor; I'd be confident to leave Heidi with them...their girls would love it. What about Daniel and Tim? I'm sure my parents would be delighted to have them for us...

So our pipe-dream materialised. The easily-used concepts of relaxing

Our week in The Gambia was another significant step back to something like normal life

and unwinding took on a whole new reality. We became aware of just how tightly the last six months had coiled us. Our week in The Gambia was another significant step back to something like normal life. Once again people had put themselves out to help us, and the whole family felt the benefit.

Since Heidi had been home after her operation, Kate the fizzy physio had been bounding in about once a fortnight, and Carole the teacher had been calling each week. The first few months of Heidi's life had done nothing for the poor muscle tone that is characteristic of babies with Down's syndrome, or for her general development. She had missed some of the important early progress and we now needed to try to make up for lost time.

Kate and Carole gave us complementary programmes of exercises for Heidi to stimulate her mental and physical development. The approach was to prepare her to reach the standard milestones that normal children achieve naturally. Hopefully with this assistance she would not be too far behind. Carole spent many hours on her knees patiently encouraging Heidi to look at a mirror, or hold a rattle. Early targets were to focus on a brightly coloured toy, then follow it from side to side, then reach out for it. Carole shook and banged toys above Heidi to encourage her to raise her head when lying on her tummy. She placed objects just out of reach so Heidi had to move to get them. At about six months Kate provided a soft 'tumble form' chair so Heidi could sit fairly upright. This enabled Heidi to learn to bang toys on a table, a skill I sometimes felt could have usefully been left untaught! Heidi loved these weekly sessions and her friend Carole seemed equally enthusiastic.

Big brother Tim was often around and was naturally intrigued by the proceedings. He was very keen to 'help' Heidi with her tasks. My role was to distract him by reading endless books, while still taking in and remembering the exercises to repeat and repeat and repeat during the coming week. Each term Carole prepared a detailed list of activites, so I always had this to fall back on if my memory failed.

It was a constant struggle to squeeze the exercises into hours which seemed far shorter than they used to be. When I failed to do so I felt I was letting Heidi down and that if she failed to fulfil her potential it would be my fault. When I succeeded I often felt depressed; her poor floppy limbs seemed so slow to fill out and strengthen despite so much attention. Her targets sometimes seemed like specks on the horizon which never came closer.

Yet as she grew more able to express herself, her ready smile and laugh would soon cheer me up. When she finally did manage some small thing, to grab a toy or roll over or sit up, the long weeks of frustration fruited in an intense joy at her great achievement.

A speech therapist also came sometimes. Her first task was to get Heidi to drink so she could be weaned from her tube. Like talking, it is all to do with making the right shape with your mouth. You probably don't know how many different shapes, sizes and designs of bottle teats and feeder cups are available, because most babies aren't too bothered. We amassed what was probably the most valuable collection in the world, but to no avail. Heidi was quite happy eating cereals, bananas or cauliflower, but give her a bottle to suck and she didn't want to know, whether the teat was shaped like a nipple or an elephant's trunk.

As a result Heidi was nearly a year old before the pump and tube were finally jettisoned and the speech therapist was able to concentrate on speech.

'Encourage listening and copying sounds which you and Heidi enjoy', as she put it. I sometimes felt I was approaching the limits of my mental tether, but I am thankful to say that Heidi's pleasure in saying 'oo ah ba ba da da' appeared greater than mine.

Two wallies and another baby

Spring 1996 and my thoughts were turning towards another baby. The prospect had been bubbling away in the back of my mind since Steve had made that rash remark on the day Heidi was born. He was not going to be allowed to forget it. At first it had been another guilt-tripping way to escape from reality. I had been thinking about another child as a replacement for the damaged goods I had unwrapped; the next one would be the perfect daughter Heidi should have been.

Was I still thinking like that underneath, I worried sometimes, especially when I was exhausted from a frustrating session with an unresponsive Heidi.

'Is it wrong to want another baby?' I asked Steve.

'Not necessarily,' he replied cautiously, knowing what was coming up, but honesty preventing him from being too negative.

'When I think about it, I always visualise a daughter who will be like I wanted Heidi to be; and then I feel bad. It seems as if I can't really have accepted her if I want another one.'

'But you don't want to replace her, do you. It's not as if you're going to trade her in for the new improved model.'

'No, I can't bear to think of losing her now. I love her so much.'

'You have accepted her for who she is, then, haven't you', Steve replied gently. 'That doesn't make it wrong to want another child to love for who she is, or he is.'

'You did say "Heidi doesn't have to be the last one now".'

'You've made sure the words are burned into my brain, dear.' Not quite so gentle now. He quickly went on: 'But there's no hurry, you've got so much to cope with. Daniel's not even four yet and Heidi will be very hard work for a long time yet. You wouldn't want another baby when Heidi is still like a baby herself.' Amazing how concerned he is for my welfare sometimes.

'They do take nine months, you know. And I might take a few months to get pregnant, and…'

'That would be a first.'

'As I was saying before I was so rudely interrupted, the others are only about eighteen months apart. I wouldn't want her… I mean I wouldn't want the baby to be all on its own, much younger than the others.'

'I wasn't suggesting waiting five years. Heidi will develop more slowly anyway. The next one will catch her up, so it would be a good thing to wait a bit longer'.

Ouch. That was something I was dreading already. I had to grudgingly admit, in my more rational moments, that Steve's arguments made sense. But I hate waiting for things. Now I'd started thinking about it, I wanted to get on with it.

Eventually Steve was wearied by my persistence, like the unjust judge in the parable Jesus told:

'Oh, all right then'. *Yes!*

By now it was summer. Very soon I had some good news to tell Steve, which elicited a predictable 'I told you so.' But my excitement was mingled with a deep fear.

'I hope the baby's all right', I would say to Steve.

'You know Heidi hasn't got the hereditary form of Down's syndrome. There is only a slightly increased risk for subsequent pregnancies. It is incredibly improbable to have two babies with Down's.'

'I know the statistics', I wailed, 'but I just can't help worrying about it.'

Steve put a comforting arm around me. 'I know. But we have proved God is faithful over the last year or so. We must try to trust him with this baby. He won't let us suffer more than we are able to bear, he has promised that in the Bible.'

I had to have one 'consultant appointment' during the pregnancy. I was dreading this, because he was sure to ask me about the Alpha Foetal Protein (AFP) blood test. This tests for 'foetal abnormalities', to use the cold medical terminology. I had always refused this test. If it doesn't come back clear it shows a 'potential problem'. It never deals in certainties. It's always 'one chance in fifty of having spina bifida' or 'one in 300 of having Down's syndrome', or whatever the probability might be of having a 'substandard' baby. If there is a possibility of Down's syndrome, the next stage is an amniocentesis, to confirm or deny the AFP's findings. This is an invasive procedure in which a needle is inserted into the uterus to draw out the amniotic fluid for testing. This procedure carries a 1% risk of inducing miscarriage, due in part to the possibility of inserting the needle into the baby.

'Mrs Bloggs, the blood test shows an increased risk of Down's syndrome, about one in 200', the doctor says. 'I assume you will want us to perform an amniocentesis'.

He should add, 'This procedure is very successful. 95% of children with Down's are eliminated as a result of it. We cause four perfectly healthy children to be miscarried for every Down's child we detect, but still, no pain, no gain, eh!' (according to a study at St Bartholomew's hospital)

The only 'cure' for Down's syndrome and other 'foetal abnormalities' is termination of pregnancy; the destruction of a life created by God in his image, even if not up to society's standards. So there had never seemed much point in having the AFP test.

I had asked my GP to put in my notes that I did not want it. There had been no pressure at the twelve week scan when it would normally have taken place, but I feared the gynaecologist would not leave it at that.

'Mrs Crowter', I imagined him saying, 'one child with Down's syndrome is enough for anyone. Don't you think you have been a little foolish in refusing the AFP? It's too late for the AFP now, but we could go straight on to an amniocentesis. I think you should seriously consider it'.

I had been praying that I wouldn't be pressurised about it, but it was still with some trepidation that I went in to the room. As usual, although it was a consultant appointment, I would only get to see his sidekick. I hadn't seen the doctor before, but his smile was friendly as I surveyed him warily.

'Mrs Crowter', he said. 'That's an unusual name. Is your husband's name Steve?'

I looked up, startled. What did they teach at medical schools these days, mind-reading?

'Yes, it is, actually.'

'Did he go to school in Kingston?'

'Yes, he did.' It was becoming, I imagined, a bit like a visit to Gypsy Rose Lee, but with more accuracy and without the palm-tickling nonsense.

'I was at school with him. What's he up to these days?'

We started chatting and immediately the tension slid away.

'I see from your notes that you didn't have the AFP test. You know all about it do you?'

I explained my reasons for not having it. He would have known what Steve's views on abortion were, so he was not at all surprised. There was no attempt to persuade me otherwise, nor the least implication that I was foolish.

I went home with a great sense of relief. God has many ways of answering prayer and I really appreciated that one.

It was an ongoing struggle to trust God and not worry, although the pregnancy progressed smoothly. I was delighted to feel the baby moving and kicking, but I would rapidly become concerned if it had a rest. I became like a crazed sergeant major, expecting a twenty four hours a day exercise regime. With the benefit of hindsight I knew Heidi had been less active than the others, so I was very sensitised to the movement of this one.

Finally the time came and we were making that familiar journey once more. Now it was so close my fears were pressing in on me again. I couldn't wait until it was over. Hopefully it wouldn't be too long, being a fourth child.

But my hope was far from fulfilled. The contractions stopped as soon as we arrived and we ended up wandering around the hospital for half the morning, hoping the movement would get things going again. Eventually we made it to the delivery room, but after four hours in there I was beginning to panic.

'Is everything all right?'

'Yes, it's fine', the midwife replied soothingly. My worries, though, would not be quelled. Was she just trying to keep me calm? She seemed to be paying a lot of attention to the monitor showing the baby's heart rate. *This isn't right, there must be something wrong with the baby...hang on, I think it's coming at last ... yes ...*

'Has it got Down's syndrome?' I blurted.

'It's a girl!'

'HAS IT GOT DOWN'S SYNDROME?'

'She doesn't have any of the characteristics of Down's syndrome. You've got nothing to worry about', said the midwife calmly. At last, after all these months of having that thought gnawing away, I was free. Deep relief washed over me with the exhaustion.

'Did you say it's a girl?' Now I could appreciate it. I held Suzanna close and looked into her eyes. The last lagging doubts drained away as I saw for myself that it was true. I took her little legs in my hand. They were firm and strong. I unrolled the fingers wrapped tightly around mine. No unbroken crease across the tiny palm. *Thank you, Lord.* 'It's just what I wanted' has never rung more true. Now my family really was complete. Not the one I'd imagined, but the one God had chosen for me and with which I was perfectly happy.

'Now I know why she was such a long time coming'. The midwife was holding up an umbilical cord with a knot in the middle. 'This is what we call a true knot. It's not just a loop. See how tight it is. It makes it harder for the oxygen to get through to the baby. I was getting concerned that she was becoming unreactive towards the end, as if she was going to sleep. I was only seconds away from taking you for an emergency Caesarian when she finally decided to arrive.' So she **had** been putting on the 'no worries' line. Steve and I smiled weakly at each other, even more thankful now for the safe birth of our daughter.

'It's very rare'. The midwife was still holding the cord. 'Do you mind if I take it to show my student?'

Despite the complications Suzanna and I both made a rapid recovery. Later on a nurse came to ask if I would like to go home or stay in hospital for the night.

'I'll get more peace here if I can have a room on my own', I replied. 'If I'm on a ward I won't sleep at all, so I'd rather go home.'

There was a room available but I still had a bad night. I couldn't blame Suzanna; she slept very well. The problem was that I kept waking up, and every time was unable to believe what my befuddled brain was telling me. I had to get out of bed, go over to the cot and check that she really was a healthy little girl.

Steve came the next day with the others. The boys, of course, rushed in full of excitement. But as I saw Heidi being carried in Steve's arms the reality of the situation suddenly struck me like a fist in my sensitive solar plexus. What have I let myself in for? A brand new baby, and another one who still can't walk! Why hadn't I listened to Steve?

I didn't have long to panic because they were all over Suzanna, grabbing, stroking... 'Those are Suzanna's eyes, Heidi, no, don't poke them'...patting, hugging... 'Be gentle, Heidi, she's not a teddy bear'...kissing, touching... 'Those are her ears, Heidi, DON'T PULL THEM'...

'Those are Suzanna's eyes, Heidi, no, don't poke them'...

For the first time in her life Heidi seemed big as she explored her wonderful new toy, grasping the tiny fingers in her huge chubby fist, threatening to squeeze the life out of Suzanna's delicate form as she enveloped her delightedly in a sisterly hug.

Steve was telling me what had happened after he had left me the day before and gone to collect the boys from their temporary guardians:

'When I told the boys the news, Tim rushed off yelling excitedly, 'We've got a baby sister and her name's Hosanna!''

I laughed happily at the delicious mistake. We both felt like singing loud hosannas of praise to our God for his perfect gift. *With God's help, we'll cope with our four little bundles of trouble and joy,* I thought contentedly.

We only became aware of the full significance of the umbilical cord knot a few days later when I was back at home. I was recounting my birth experience to the visiting midwife. Her eyes widened in surprise.

'Was it a true knot?'

'Yes'.

'Wow, someone was looking after you.'

She told us that the knot becomes tighter and tighter as the baby moves around. Often this restricts the blood flow so much that the baby dies or is brain-damaged. I looked down at my precious, perfect daughter. Yes, Someone certainly had been looking after us and her.

Casualties

Yet once more Heidi and I were making the familiar trip to Birmingham. The car was on autopilot and my thoughts were free to roam. It was two years since Heidi's operation and time for another six-monthly check-up. Yes, this was just a routine visit and Heidi seemed to be in good health. There was no reason to worry, and yet my adrenaline level was up. It was partly an automatic response to driving this route; yet it was more than that. What if they found a problem? I couldn't bear to think about it; neither could I help thinking about it.

'Mrs Crowter, please come through'. At last the wait was over. I took the seat the consultant indicated and awaited the verdict.

'I'm delighted to say Heidi is in very good shape.' I exhaled the tension as he continued. 'There is still a little leakage from one of the valves, but it's nothing to worry about. She shouldn't be needing another operation for the foreseeable future. In fact, I don't think we need to see her again for two years.'

Suddenly I felt exultant. Every six months had implied some degree of concern about Heidi's heart; there was always an appointment looming. The fear that she might need that second operation had always been there. Two years was almost a discharge.

'Thank you for all you have done for her, doctor.'

In a sense it was the end of an era. My mind ran back over the past two and a half years of involvement with the hospital. Heidi had been given nothing but love, respect and the best treatments available. Thanks to that I still had my daughter. *Thank you, Lord.*

I had every reason to thank God, because such an experience is by no means universal. Sadly, many parents of children with Down's syndrome have to deal with prejudice and ignorance from the medical profession, even now. The Down's Syndrome Association (DSA) recently carried out a survey of 1,509 members. 28% reported a high level of dissatisfaction with attitudes amongst medical professionals to people with Down's syndrome. Here are some extracts from the replies:

'When first born we were told by a doctor that it would have been better if she had died at birth.'

'The ophthalmologist said: 'We won't bother with glasses as he's not what you would call university material.''

'When James was two and a half, hearing and sight problems gave rise to comments from professionals that, 'as he was mentally handicapped anyway, it didn't matter if he could see or hear properly.''

'When Daniel had his first heart operation he was in a lot of pain. We were told by staff when we asked for pain relief, 'Oh, he has Down's syndrome; they don't feel any pain.''

'Our son was described by a Senior Physician as 'an unacceptable burden on resources medically, socially and educationally.''

'I was told by our original paediatric consultant that it would cost at least £10,000 for heart surgery and that they would rather spend that sort of money on a 'normal' child.'

As the DSA concluded: 'It is clear that many medical staff are failing to adhere to existing guidelines and that their prejudice and ignorance is affecting the care that people with Down's syndrome are offered. Horrifyingly though, it is evident that in some cases, lives are being put at risk.'

The case of Joanne Harris gained great publicity in 2000. For some years she and her mother had struggled, and failed, to persuade the Health Authority to allow her to have the heart transplant she needed. Finally they tried to raise funds to enable her to have the operation in America. Then a friend won the first Big Brother television competition and donated his £80,000 prize to her fund. Suddenly the Health Authority found she could have the operation here after all. In an instant all their previous arguments about the high risk and extra complications became surmountable. Not for humanitarian reasons, of course, but due to a dislike of negative publicity.

We like to see ourselves as a 'developed', 'civilised' country. Surely a distinguishing mark of a truly civilised country is that it shows extra concern for those who are disadvantaged. They should get the best treatment, not the fag end. This sometimes requires extra resources, but civilisation is about people, not wealth. To write off those who need the most help on grounds of cost or prejudice is barbaric. We may recoil from the comparison, but how many steps is that attitude removed from Hitler's eugenic philosophy?

The pre-school maze

'I love the sound of Heidi's laugh. Life would be so dull without her, wouldn't it. We'd just wake up in the morning and think 'Oh well, another dull old Monday''.

Tim's unprompted comment neatly encapsulated the extra dimension Heidi brings to our everyday family life. Life is rarely easy, but it is certainly never dull. I thought back to the seemingly interminable process leading up to Heidi starting school. By turns frustrating, depressing, wearing. And yet lightened by Heidi's unfailing cheerfulness and enthusiasm; and the caring commitment of so many of her professional helpers.

The scenario had seemed so clear cut with the boys; when the time came they went to playgroup, then school. It just happened, there were no issues or complications. With Heidi, the saga began much earlier. She started nursery when she was about a year old, so before then we had to decide where she should go. Heidi's teacher Carole took me to see the different options, and the choice we made proved an excellent one. It was a mainstream nursery, but the two sessions each week Heidi attended were for children with special needs. Her band of professional helpers were able to go in and see her there, often having group sessions with others of their 'clients' who also attended the nursery. I appreciated these periods of respite even more after Suzie arrived on the scene. The pressure to practice Heidi's various exercises was also eased by the knowledge that the dedicated nursery staff were filling her time there so positively, using the programmes provided by her professionals and other stimulating activities.

Carole still came to visit Heidi at home too. By now they had moved on to posting, first balls and then shapes. Over the next year they did three, four, then five piece jigsaws. They rolled a ball to each other, although sometimes the roll would turn into a throw and Carole would become a target. They practiced language using picture cards; recognising, then pointing, then copying the sounds. Carole's target sheets became Individual Educational Plans, running to five or six A4 sheets of specific exercises designed to work towards Heidi's targets. These would cover all developmental areas:

Language and Literacy (e.g. pointing to body parts). Heidi's speech therapist also called every six weeks or so and worked on this area in conjunction with Carole.

Mathematics (e.g. Building a tower of three bricks).

Physical (e.g. Walking holding someone's hand).

Personal and Social Development (e.g. Pouring water).

Carole meticulously recorded Heidi's progress, or lack of it, in each activity week by week. By the age of two Heidi was beginning to say a few words and walking with a baby walker, legs wide apart due to her continuing muscle weakness. It was a long process to train those legs to straighten. She chose Christmas Day 1997, before an admiring audience of cousins, uncles, aunts and grandparents, to take her first solo steps. Revelling in the reaction this produced, she carried on right across the room. It had taken two and a half years, but after that there was no stopping her.

In January, Heidi started going to the playgroup the boys had been to, as well as her two mornings at the special needs nursery. The leader was delighted to take her, true to her word to me in those first weeks of Heidi's life. She was the first child with Down's to go there, but they were more than happy to make the extra effort necessary. It was another opportunity for Heidi's stimulation, progress and fun.

Almost immediately it was time to start making decisions again, this time regarding the nursery for her pre-school year starting in September. It seemed impossible this could be coming around so soon, but being born in July meant she would be one of the youngest in her year. She could go to the nursery attached to a school for children with moderate learning difficulties. The natural progression from here would be to move on to that school, although that did not have to happen. The main alternative was a new service called an Enhanced Resource Nursery. This was a mainstream nursery, but with provision for six children with special needs among the twenty or so others. The success of this system was subsequently illustrated by the comment of another prospective parent bring shown around:

'It looks very good, but where are the children with special needs?'

Heidi's teacher, Carole

In effect the decision was not just for the coming year, but possibly for the whole of Heidi's school life. Did we want her to go to a special needs school? Classes would be small. The whole system would be designed with special needs pupils in mind. She would be working with children of a similar ability level. The school had a good reputation.

Once again Carole took me to see the two nurseries. I was impressed with both, but which would be the best for Heidi ? We wanted her to be fully integrated in society one day; surely it was best to start the process as soon as possible. Another line of thought was that Heidi was always observing and imitating others. This was often a good thing, although it did mean she picked up the boys' bad habits. In a mainstream environment we hoped that her development would be helped by copying others, but in a special school the opposite could happen. Mainstream classes would be larger, true, but she would have a Special Needs Assistant.

Our thoughts were beginning to settle, but a nagging thought disturbed me. From her earliest days my mental picture, at positive times, had been of Heidi going to our local school with the others. I wanted her to be normal, not bussing off to a special school halfway across the city. Was I really focussed on fulfilling Heidi's needs, or was I rationalising the pros and cons in order to fulfil mine?

We needed some external input. We found various articles and research studies on inclusion of children with Down's and were pleased to find that their conclusions were the same as ours. The evidence of two major UK research studies seemed conclusive; children in mainstream schools performed better in all the measured attainment criteria. Differing abilities at the outset were allowed for in the studies. This settled our minds and we put Heidi forward for a place at the enhanced nursery. For her first year at school she would need a Statement of Special Educational Needs prepared by the Education Service. Our aim was that this would recommend Heidi for a place at our local mainstream school. I was heartened to find the school extremely positive about having her.

As usual, Heidi was very excited at the prospect of a new experience. She settled into the nursery immediately, enthusiastically joining in with everything (except waiting for her turn); watching and copying when she didn't know what to do.

There were complications, of course, mostly to do with her size. She is still tiny; on the Down's height chart her best ever effort is the third centile. Out of a hundred Down's children her age, she would be in the smallest three. She doesn't have the same difficulty on the weight chart, that's usually around the fiftieth centile. But she could not reach most of the activities at the nursery. Her physiotherapist sent in a special chair and stool to enable her to participate. Another by-product of her smallness is shown by this comment from her first report: 'Heidi is very popular with all the children and she has to be rescued from those who are delighted to put her to bed all day'.

Our favourite remark in her report was this: 'Heidi's special strength must be her lovely sunny personality and sense of humour'. As we considered the next stage in her life, we hoped that this defining aspect of her character would continue to flourish. We prayed that it would not be stunted by a growing awareness of her disabilities, or through experiencing cruelty from others.

This next stage was school, and by March the dreaded Statementing process was beginning. The Statement would consist of a detailed description of Heidi's special educational needs; and an equally specific list of the special educational provisions and staffing skills necessary to meet them. It would also describe any non-educational needs such as health problems. It would contain recommendations as to school placement and any extra arrangements required to meet Heidi's non-educational needs.

In order to prepare this document, reports were required from Heidi's nursery, paediatrician, speech therapist, physiotherapist, audiologist, educational psychologist and us. This necessitated endless meetings and assessments. Inevitably all the reports were not in by the deadline; some were a month late. Despite my chivvying, the delay was passed down the line and the Statement was not produced on time. My concern was that Heidi's Special Needs Assistant would be appointed in time. The school could not appoint the position until the official confirmation came in the Statement. It would be horrible if Heidi could not start school with the other children because she had no assistant.

It seems a common experience that parents of children with special needs learn to be pushy on their behalf. Steve says that comes more easily to some than others. I'm not sure I know what he means by that. Anyway, after I sent off a stroppy fax, the draft Statement appeared with remarkable alacrity. We were thankful to find we were happy with it and did not need to request any amendments. Unfortunately it was still too late for the school to advertise the post, so we spent the summer hoping they would be able to make an interim arrangement. Despite this loose end, it was a huge relief to come to the end of a long, hard struggle.

But other parents we knew or heard about were having a far tougher time than we had. Some schools were still very unwilling to take such children when it came to it, whatever their prospectuses might say. Some education authorites were far less pro-integration than ours. In God's plan our local authority had been criticised a few years before by a government report on its approach to integration. The result is that it now has one of the highest levels of integration in the country.

So, even if this was just a lull before the beginning of the next long, hard struggle, there were good reasons to be thankful for progress so far and encouraged as we contemplated the future.

Heidi settled into the nursery immediately

Educating Heidi

We had wondered if this day would ever arrive. Heidi had fought her way through quite a few stages of her personal assault course to reach this momentous point. That first few months, when she was too concerned with merely staying alive to make any developmental progress. The repeated bouts of pneumonia over her first winter. Her painstaking struggle to make up for that lost opportunity, all the while dragged back by the ball and chain of her physical and mental impairments.

After becoming lost several times in the maze of the Statementing process, we could at last see the 'EXIT' sign looming. The school was happy to welcome her for the beginning of term, although her assistant had not yet been appointed.

So here she was, resplendent in her school uniform, just the same as the boys'. 'Room to grow' was putting it kindly, but she was so proud. It was quite a struggle to get her to sit still for long enough to take the obligatory first day photo, but there was no need to say 'cheese.' A huge grin was fixed more firmly on her face than the rictus you get on your wedding day.

Will she be all right? She seems so tiny in her uniform, not big enough for school. She's only just four. Will she cope? I hope they've got a temporary assistant organised for her.

The moment of truth arrived. I didn't want to let go of her hand, but Heidi didn't share my apprehensions. She pulled herself away and bounded in delightedly to meet her new friends.

I was relieved to discover a Special Needs Educational Assistant in place. I recognised her as a fellow parent.

'Come in and tell me a bit about Heidi', she said. I didn't want to tell her too much for fear that she would become a very temporary assistant. As we chatted Heidi was becoming acquainted with her new environment; washing the sleeves of her pristine jumper in the water play area and checking out the sand to see if it tasted any better than the stuff at home. I realised from her reaction that Debbie Hemming was not going to be fazed by Heidi's idiosyncrasies.

Thankfully Mrs Hemming was going to fill in on a regular basis until the creaking wheels of Local Education Authority bureaucracy had completed their rotation and a permanent appointment was made. We had been concerned that it would be unsettling for Heidi to be continually having different helpers, or, worse still, none at all. We soon discovered that Mrs Hemming was the ideal assistant, enthusiastic, loving and firm. We hoped she would apply for the permanent job, and were delighted when she was eventually appointed. The school's Special Educational Needs Co-ordinator, Karen Fenlon, was Heidi's class teacher, so we could not have wanted a better team.

Heidi quickly adapted to her new routine. She has never been fazed by change, taking great pleasure in each new experience. Because of her small stature and heart condition she still tired easily, so she only went to school in the mornings. We need not have been concerned that this would prevent her becoming a fully paid-up member of the class. She became extremely popular, although some of her classmates had to be dissuaded from treating her like a living doll. She soon seemed to know the name of nearly everyone in the school.

'Good mornin' Ryan. Good mornin' Emily.' It was a long haul to cross the playground each morning, like being on walkabout with the Queen.

She kept being stopped for a conversation as she walked along the corridor or sat in the library doing one-to-one work with Mrs Hemming. This was creating so many distractions from her work that the children had to be asked to stop doing it.

'Just treat her like any other child'. It was a good aim which has gradually been achieved, but many of the children have a special affection for her. Even grunting, uncooperative eleven year old boys are transformed into angels of mercy in her presence.

'Come on Heidi, take a penalty!'

Never mind the fact that she would need at least ten kicks to reach the goal, the lads were determined she would have a go.

'Well done Heidi, brilliant goal!' Inevitably the goalkeeper had contrived to miss completely his exaggerated attempt at a save. Heidi revelled in the celebrations and attention.

The penalty competition was part of a charity fund-raising event at the school. As usual Heidi was taking maximum enjoyment from the occasion. As soon as we had got through the gate, a swarm of chaperones had descended to remove her from us and escort her around the stalls.

'Heidi, here you are, I bought this for you.' *Marvellous, yet another teddy for our collection.*

'Heidi, have a go at the table football.' Not only did she win her match but the whole competition. The test match cricket authorities would have been appalled at such blatant match fixing, but she walked away with the prize without so much as an internal enquiry.

Her class's performance of 'Goldilocks and the Three Bears' was one of her first opportunities to tread the boards. Predictably, she was not exactly overcome with stage fright. She was a flower, but was not going to be content with a non-speaking part. Noticing the approval of the audience when she continued her dance after the other flowers had stepped down, she took every opportunity to add her own ad hoc contributions to the script.

'Who's been eating my porridge?'

'It was her!' yelled Heidi, rushing onto the stage and pointing an accusing finger at Goldilocks.

The procession out at the end took rather longer than normal because she had to shake hands or touch the knees of most of the parents sitting by the aisle.

A number of the children and mums came up to me afterwards.

'Your little girl was the star of the show.' 'Isn't Heidi coming on well.' 'She brought the house down.' 'I'm so glad she's come here—it's really good for the school.' 'Mixing kids with Down's syndrome in mainstream schools is a great idea.'

Of course, Heidi's contributions did not always go down so well. When two boys were sent out of assembly for talking, she shouted out:

'Shh, shh, go to your classrooms!' Then more quietly at intervals throughout the rest of the assembly:

'I'm a good girl, I am.'

Eventually she learned to sit still and quiet with the other children. One day she proudly brought home her first certificate of achievement, for 'Sitting still and listening in assembly.' However, her assertions of goodness were not always backed up by her behaviour in class. When I went to pick Heidi up I would usually be forewarned by two or three children before being approached by a solemn Miss Fenlon or Mrs Hemming to be told of the day's misdemeanours.

'I found Heidi with both hands down the toilet and toilet paper all over the floor.' Her face was severe, but Heidi was standing beside her, head cocked to one side, looking up at her with a big grin. I struggled to keep my face straight.

'It's not funny is it, Heidi', Mrs Hemming was saying.

'Yes, it is.'

'You won't do it again, will you?'

'Yes.' This was probably true, but perhaps not the best answer. Suzie would watch these exchanges and absorb them with avid interest.

'Heidi was a very naughty girl at school today', she would say at dinner time, and with great relish she would regale Steve with all the juicy details.

It was slow going, but gradually Heidi realised that we and her teachers were not going to let her get away with hair-pulling or eating various unmentionable substances or pushing her classmates. Immature forms of behaviour such as these are a part of her delayed development, but she is perfectly capable of learning to behave in acceptable ways. It would be failing her if we let them pass with an apologetic 'It's because she's got Down's syndrome' and we were pleased to find that her teachers shared our philosophy.

With so much stimulation her speech came on well, with longer and more complex sentences. She started including more linking words. She hadn't bothered with them before because she could make herself understood without them. Alongside books from a reading scheme she was given key words on flash cards. By the end of her first term she could recognise about thirty-five words when she was in the mood. She would proudly bring her reading books home to show us. Suzie was very interested and would ask Heidi what the words said. It delighted Heidi (and us) to be of superior knowledge and teach them to her sister.

The rest of the class were, of course, on a steeper learning curve. We were so pleased with her progress it was easy to forget that she was learning much more slowly than the others. It was a jolting reminder to look around the classroom on parents' evenings and see the evidence staring down from the walls. It cheered us up to discover that she could read more words than some of her classmates, so at least she was keeping up in one area, so far. We feared even this would not last much longer.

After the novelty of reading had worn off, Heidi would sometimes be lazy and claim not to be able to read her books. On one occasion she tripped herself up. Pointing to the next word, she said:

'I don't know that word 'and!''

Her first year soon drew towards its close, and Sports Day arrived. Heidi thoroughly enjoyed taking part in each activity. She is one of the few people who still subscribe to the dog-eared dictum 'It's not winning, it's taking part that counts.' It's a good thing she does, or life would soon become depressing for her. My abiding image of that summer afternoon is Heidi determinedly heading for the finishing line long after the other competitors had finished, face lit by a smile of pure joy. The children lining the track were clapping and shouting 'Hei-DI, Hei-DI,' as she came in, a victor.

 'Although Heidi only scored at the first percentile (99% of same age peers would perform better than Heidi did on this occasion), she has made progress.'

The cold combination of raw statistics and standard-format wording in the speech therapy end of term review gave us a jolt of dismay. We felt she had been making good progress over her first school year; we had seen her developing. We felt the review, based on one twenty minute snapshot when Heidi had a bad cold, did not do her justice, but the stark picture given was still a discouragement.

We had no such problems with her school report.

'Heidi will spell her name correctly using magnetic letters … enthusiastic … excellent progress with her reading …enthusiastic…can count a set of ten objects with support … enthusiastic … come on in leaps and bounds … enthusiastic … delightful girl.'

Even the comments which could have been negative were couched in the wonderful language of Teacherese:

'She will sit still and listen for short periods of time, depending on how interested she is in the stimulus on offer.' Interpretation: After about thirty seconds she gets up and wanders off.

'She understands the importance of listening to others and is beginning to do this more frequently.' Interpretation: She still usually prefers talking.

'Heidi has a natural curiosity for her immediate environment and has enjoyed investigating and exploring within it.' Interpretation: She will immediately spot and grab anything messy and shove it in her mouth/ears/hair.

'She is beginning to develop more of a spatial awareness and is becoming more responsive to simple instructions.' Interpretation: She is not quite so clumsy as she was and occasionally does as she is told.

End of term; time to reflect on the year. There had been so many concerns and unknowns at the outset. Would our tiny tot be able to cope with 'big school'? Would she be picked on or laughed at? Would her placement in a group of mainstream ability children just throw her limitations into depressingly sharp focus? Integration is not always successful. We knew of another mainstream school where a boy with special needs faced the possibility of being uprooted.

'We want to make a success of it', his teacher and assistant would say, but seemed unwilling to make that extra effort required.

Despite the initial pangs of anxiety, we had been convinced that integration was the best solution for Heidi. Our conviction had strengthened further during the year as we had observed her progress. We could look back with satisfaction, but it hadn't just 'happened'. The school had been wholly positive from the outset. Karen Fenlon and Debbie Hemming had been totally committed to Heidi and determined to do everything they could for her. These were essential ingredients for which we were deeply thankful.

But what of the rest of the school? How many people with Down's syndrome and other disabilities have suffered at the hands or tongues of people who do not have to live with their disadvantages? And how many of those incidences of prejudice are due to ignorance? Three hundred or so children had experienced Heidi this year. The vast majority had grown to appreciate her sameness and her difference. Surely those children who had laughed at her show-off stage performances and showered her with a seemingly endless stream of Christmas cards would not now grow up with hearts and minds closed to people like Heidi. They would be far more likely to accept and respect people for who they are, because ignorance had been overcome.

So now we could look back with great thankfulness on many fears allayed and countless prayers answered. Yes, there had been sad moments, but many happy, fulfilling hours. Our caring Father was still looking after his Heidi.

'It's not funny is it, Heidi.' Special needs assistant, Debbie Hemming was not going to be fazed by Heidi's idiosyncrasies

The obligatory first school day photo

Sister act

'Hello, what's your name?' We were at the doctor's surgery again and Heidi was making herself known in the waiting room. These visits were frequent, but never monotonous.

'Can you speak French?' On our recent holiday soon after her sixth birthday Heidi had become fascinated with the language.

'No, I can't.'

'I can. Un, deux, trois, quatre, cinq, six, sept, huit, neuf, dix.'

'I wish I could do that', replied the lady, suitably impressed.

'Yes'. Then she was off again 'Un, deux trois…'

'I only wish she'd learnt to count in English so quickly', I said to the lady. It was a heartfelt comment; the process had seemed interminable. The thought took me back to one of those saddening moments when reality strikes home.

'Come on Heidi, count with me. 'One, two…'

'Four, eight, six, five,' Heidi joined in with great confidence.

'No, let's try again. One, two…'

'Nine, three, seven, six…' She had known the numbers for months. Why couldn't she count properly? I took a deep breath.

'Let's try again, Heidi. One, two…'

'One two three four five six seven eight nine ten,' carolled a cheerful little voice. I looked up in surprise at Suzie's grinning face framed in the doorway. She was just learning numbers. The other day she could only count to three.

The scenario was one which had been casting its lengthening shadow over us for some time. There was a grim inevitability about it, like that date with the dentist gleefully circled in red on the calendar by one's wife. For the last six months or so the two of them had been broadly comparable, Heidi ahead with reading, writing and numbers; Suzie much more quick and co-ordinated physically and with clearer speech. But now, Suzie was three and a quarter and loving the nursery she had just started going to. Numbers were swiftly mastered and before long letters would follow.

Чeidi and Suzie are great friends

We had been delighted when Heidi had started to write her name during her previous school year. After much effort and practice she had learned the 'H'. 'I' and 'd' had followed eventually, but 'e' seemed beyond her. She would just leave gaps for someone else to fill them in. Now, some months later, 'e' still seemed an insurmountable obstacle.

One day Suzie announced 'I want to write my name.' Half an hour later she had got it, Heidi's nemesis 'e' having been vanquished without a murmur. We had been so conditioned by constant repetition and reinforcement with Heidi that we had forgotten how easily and naturally a normal child picks things up.

It is a strange experience to be sad when your child makes progress. Yes, it is mixed with pleasure and pride, but it is sometimes an effort to be enthusiastic when it throws Heidi's limitations into such sharp relief. It is, of course, an effort that has to be made, to avoid being unfair to Suzie. But the unalloyed pleasure such achievements brought with the boys is missing as Suzie increasingly overtakes Heidi in so many areas, with the effortlessness of a Ferrari powering past a dawdling truck.

By this time Suzie had a definite height advantage too, although Heidi was still a division or two up in the weight department. For the past year or so they had always been taken for twins by strangers. The response 'No, this one's three and that one's five', was usually met with the sort of look which said 'There's either something wrong with my ears or your brain, and I think it's the latter.' It always gave me a pang of sadness; another sign of Heidi's 'big sisterhood' being denied by her Down's syndrome. But the subsequent explanation sometimes led on to further conversation. People would be amazed to hear what Heidi had been through, giving a natural opportunity to share our faith.

'So many people were praying for her through that time. We're quite sure that God answered those prayers, because only he could have healed her.'

Suzie was not slow to make the most of this new-found opportunity to score points.

'I'm big and you're small, Heidi'.

'No, I'm big and you're small, Suzie.'

In an effort to bring some sense into this oft-rehearsed futility, Liz said one day:

'God made everyone different, girls. Some people are big and some are small.' So next time Suzie opened with the Pious Gambit:

'God made me big and you small, Heidi'. It doesn't take a Kasparov to work out how the game continued, but Heidi wasn't going to concede without a fight.

On a school outing a couple of days later she was in an unfamiliar toilet.

'Careful when you get down, it's rather high,' warned Mrs Hemming.

'It's all right', replied Heidi calmly from her precarious perch. 'God made me big.'

Heidi and Suzie are great friends and mostly play very well together. Their constant communication and imaginative games have certainly brought Heidi on in her development. But sometimes Suzie's bossiness is a bit hard to take. She soon noticed that we would praise Heidi for doing things that she herself could achieve quite easily. She decided she would help with Heidi's education.

'Here you are Heidi, can you put your socks on?' An excessive round of applause would ensue when Heidi good-naturedly obliged.

'Well done Heidi, good girl. You ARE clever.' Unbeknown to Suzie, this was all said in the most patronising tone imaginable. One time in the car I was severely reprimanded for failing to clap Heidi for some unspectacular achievement. Knowing Suzie, she would otherwise have torn me off a strip for removing my hands from the steering wheel.

Next Suzie moved on to correcting Heidi's pronunciation errors, real or imagined. Heidi had problems with some sounds, pronouncing 'l' like 'y' and 'r' like 'w'. She could say 's' clearly, but at this time was missing it off the beginning of words. This lazy habit had to be corrected by constant reminders to pronounce the words properly. Suzie took this a stage further by deliberately making her say appropriate words.

'What's this, Heidi?' dangling a toy before her eyes.

'It's a nake.'

'No Heidi, SSnake. Say SSnake, Heidi'

Chapter 19

'SSSnake', said Heidi obligingly.

She didn't seem to mind, but I was offended for her dignity. All at once I felt miserable and jealous. Jealous of one daughter on behalf of the other. Jealous of all those other families who just have normal children.

It was a longstanding struggle. My mind rewound once more to that moment in the hospital five years before when I had held baby William, my envy drained. Yes, it had been a real and powerful answer to my prayers. But if I had thought my problem was over, I was soon disillusioned. I had not been immunised against jealousy. My weakness is ongoing and has resurfaced at regular intervals.

'Hello Liz, how are you? Have you heard the news? Alison's had a baby girl!'

'Oh, how lovely!' My mouth asked the appropriate questions, but behind the plastic smile I was suddenly spinning again. *Why wasn't my baby normal? It's not fair! Another perfect baby at church. And it had to be a girl, didn't it.*

The strength of my reaction took me by surprise. Heidi was nine months old then, and I had thought I was getting past this sort of thing. *Haven't I really accepted her after all?*

Thankfully I haven't had such strong feelings when babies have been born since, although it still brings a twinge sometimes. But, to my shame and sadness, the right triggers can still set off an explosion.

'Now Heidi, you're all dressed again in clean, dry clothes. If you need the potty, tell me.' My voice was still calm, but my frustration was growing as high as the pile of wet clothes.

'Yes, mummy', Heidi agreed cheerfully, as though I was telling her something very obvious. Week after week this had gone on, and today was worse than ever. *She's three years old; why can't she get it? Will she ever get it?*

'Mummy, I need the potty.' She was stepping gingerly towards me, legs bowed as if she'd just dismounted after a long ride. The dark patch on her trousers was an unnecessary confirmation. *Down's syndrome. It wrecks everything!*

'We think it would be better for Heidi to go back into Reception again', the teacher was saying. Heidi had gone up with her class at the end of her first year. I had been so pleased at the review where this had been decided. Someone had said that the class would be incomplete without her.

'She is already spending quite a lot of time with the Reception class, and making good progress. She can't really do group work with the Year One class because of the gap in ability.' I had known it was coming but it didn't make it feel any better. The tears flooded when I told Steve. He did his best to cheer me up:

'She's only a couple of months older than some of the Reception children anyway, and if she's going to go down a year, it's better now than later. If she's there a lot anyway, it will be more settled to be part of the class. She'll make better progress if she can work in groups with the other children.' *Great, the voice of reason, telling me what I already know. Thanks a lot. Why does she have to have Down's syndrome?*

When I'm exhausted after a difficult day. When Heidi's limitations are shown up in comparison with another child. When she can't or won't do something that I feel she should be able to. When I stop relying on God. That's when it happens. I stamp my metaphorical foot and shake my little fist at God. *It's not fair! I don't want her to have Down's syndrome any more. Why can't she be NORMAL?*

It is a struggle from which I know I will never be free. For all her loveableness and rich character, Heidi will always have a disability. It will prevent her from doing and being some things. My challenge is to conquer those moments when my sadness turns against the God who has given us such a beautiful, different, gift.

Chapter 20

Cold feet

'Hi Liz, it's Stella from the Down's group. A girl's just had a positive amnio and she'd like to speak to someone. She's called Tracey. She's only 21. Would you go and see her?'

The sinking feeling came on as soon as I'd put the phone down. I'd volunteered to talk to new parents of Down's babies, or prospective ones. It had seemed a good idea at the time, a useful way to use my experience and hopefully help others. Now it came to it, my feet were getting decidedly chilly. *She's only just had the amniocentesis test result. She might not have decided whether to keep the baby yet.* Since the baby was labelled substandard, it was legal to have an abortion right up to birth. *What if she's waiting to see me before she makes up her mind. I'd feel terrible if she decided to have an abortion after I had spoken to her.*

I tipped my worries out on Steve.

'You can't make it sound like a bed of roses; just tell it like it is. Whatever happens, you mustn't feel guilty. It's her decision and her responsibility.'

I wonder how she's feeling. The grief, the tears, the heartache; back they came. Fresh and crisp out of cold storage, the emotions washed through me anew. It was exhausting to go through it again. I spent a night dreaming about babies with Down's syndrome being expected or born. I would be glad when it was over. I hoped Tracey wasn't thinking the same.

We told the boys about it at Bible Time so they too could pray about my visit.

'That's great—another baby with Downs!' was their immediate response.

' I could tell her what you think it's like having a sister with Down's.'

This was eight year old Daniel's verdict:

'She's priceless. I wouldn't swap her for anyone, because she's so funny and because she's my sister. Although she's had a very troubled little life, she's my sister and that's all that matters'.

Tim's answers were equally positive. He also asked me to tell Tracey about God because he was sure it would help her.

When I think of Heidi, I think of a funny but kind girl who is smiling non-stop, but what I've just written isn't nearly enough to describe Heidi. I am perfectly happy with Heidi how she is now - In fact it makes my life a lot happier. Whenever I see her I have tons less to worry about. I like games of snap with Heidi because after I shout "SNAP", she does exatly the same. "I got it before you!" She has an 'irresistable' cry that makes me want to cry with her. The happiness she nearly always shows is always inside her, even if she is crying. She always has something to cheer herself up.

By Tim

Tim's thoughts on his sister

The day came and once again my anxieties proved wasted energy. Tracey was very positive and there seemed to have been no thought of having an abortion.

'Thank you, Lord,' I said as I mulled my visit over on the way home. More prayers answered. *I hope I haven't depressed her by mentioning some negative things…here we go again. When will I learn to stop worrying?*

The boys were very keen to find out how I had got on.

'Did you tell her about God?' Tim asked immediately.

'Er, no'.

'Why not?' His face betrayed his shock and disappointment.

'There didn't seem to be a suitable moment', I replied lamely.

'Then you'll have to go back again and tell her.'

The issue was so clear to him; no unnecessary complications. Stung by my failure, I wished I could be more like that. Surely that is part of what Jesus meant when he said 'Be like little children.'

The world is not enough

Heidi's bedtime is usually a pleasure. There is the pleasant consequence of peace for the rest of the evening, but it is also a tonic in itself. A big hug, a slobbery kiss, sometimes a comment like 'I love you, you're the best daddy in the world'. It's enough to ease the strain if the evening with the children has been fractious. She is invariably happy to go to bed and takes great delight in the goodnight process, particularly the song and prayer. Her prayers, as usual, range from the ridiculous to the sublime.

'Please help Suzanna to stop makin' that racket in her bedroom. It's giving me an 'eadache.' Heidi has no problem with the concept of nothing being too small to pray about. Another time she turned to me after her prayer and said,

'I was praying to God, wasn't I. I like God. He's a nice chap.' Not theologically profound, but a little sign of a growing appreciation of important truths.

She is also very keen to take her turn to say 'grace' before meals. We sometimes have to remind the others to think about what they are saying, and come up with something more original than a mechanical 'Dear God, thank you for this lovely food. Amen.' This is never necessary with Heidi as she always has plenty of things to thank God for, or tell him about. The dinner is sometimes cold by the time she has finished, but that is a small price to pay.

One day when she was about five and a half her growing understanding crystallised into this prayer:

'Thank you for this food we have here. Help us to trust in God and Jesus. Thank you that Jesus died on the cross for our sins. Amen.' Liz dissolved into tears of pure joy and we thanked God for the simple truths of his gospel.

Soon after this we were going through a book of 'Questions and Answers' at Bible Times.

'Suzie, what was the most important thing Jesus came to do?' Suzie put on the coy look which would no doubt be put to good use in future years.

'I don't know', she whimpered helplessly.

'Died on the cross', put in Heidi. 'To save us from our sins.'

'Well done, Heidi', Liz enthused. 'There's a verse to learn too. 'Jesus came into the world to save sinners'. Can you say that, Suzie?'

Once more Suzie wasn't up to the task, but Heidi repeated it perfectly. We secretly relished the increasingly-rare opportunity for Heidi to outshine Suzie. More deeply we appreciated Heidi's unaffected enthusiasm for the truths at the heart of the Bible.

Yes, some parts of the Bible are hard to understand. But even people such as Heidi, or indeed with far more severe learning difficulties, can understand enough to be saved from their sins. Nor should we assume that they will just be 'hangers-on' in God's kingdom. They may be of more use than you or me. This story about another girl with Down's syndrome illustrates the point:

A medical consultant boarded a plane for an inner-state flight in America and he found himself sitting next to a little girl with Down's syndrome. The stewardess explained that the child was a regular passenger and there was always someone to meet her at the other end. After a minute or two the consultant was surprised when the little girl asked, 'Did you eat your breakfast this morning? My mummy says everyone should eat their breakfast.' 'Yes', the consultant responded, 'I eat breakfast every morning.' The little girl was quiet for a moment or two and then she enquired, 'Did you clean your teeth this morning? My mummy says everyone should clean their teeth.' Smilingly he assured her that he had cleaned his teeth. By this time the plane was ready to take off and the last passenger took his seat across the aisle and settled down with his newspaper. Once more the little voice interrupted, 'Do you love the Lord Jesus? My mummy says everyone should love the Lord Jesus.' The consultant replied, 'Yes indeed, I do love the Lord Jesus and I have tried to serve him all my life.' Silence once more and then, motioning with her head to the man opposite, she said, 'Ask him if he ate his breakfast this morning?' He hesitated, but the little girl insisted, 'Go on, ask him.' The consultant leaned over and apologetically explained that the little girl next to him wanted to know if he had eaten his breakfast. 'Yes, I did,' he replied. Another pause; then, 'Ask him if he cleaned his teeth this morning.' The consultant squirmed but, with a weak smile, conveyed the message and passed on the answer that the man across the aisle had cleaned his teeth. After a moment or two came the question he was dreading, 'Ask him if he loves the Lord Jesus.'

The consultant tried to explain to the little girl that that was a very personal thing and not the kind of question to ask a stranger. But she insisted, 'Go on, ask him.' He was forced to look within himself and ask why he was so reluctant to ask what is the most important question anyone could be faced with in this life. Finally, the consultant leaned over and enquired, 'The little girl wants to know if you love the Lord Jesus.' The man put down his paper and said, 'Do you know, I have heard people talk about their love for Jesus, but no one has ever really explained to me what it means.' For the rest of the flight the consultant had the opportunity to witness to this stranger about the gospel. [*Horizons of hope,* by Brian Edwards. Published by Day One Publications]

Heidi may not become a brain surgeon or strut across the world's political stage, but if she knows God, she will bring him glory in her life and enjoy his presence for ever. Such a life will be far more worthwhile than that of the most illustrious achiever who comes to the end of his life a stranger to his Creator and Judge.

Chapter 21

The bridge on the river why

'The tiny little girl called Fiona Finger was very, very ill. She was just about to die when a good fairy flew down and touched her with her wand. Fiona opened her eyes and smiled. From that moment she grew stronger and stronger and grew into a happy child who brought much joy to her parents. But sometimes they were still sad because she was too small to do everything the other children did.

'One day her mummy had another baby girl. She soon grew into a big strong child with blonde hair and blue eyes. She loved her little sister Fiona and played with her all the time. Now their mummy and daddy were really happy and they all lived happily ever after.'

I closed the book carefully to avoid waking the sleeping child…no, you're right, it's not even a real fairy story.

Six years ago, 'Why?' was the question most often on our lips and in our minds. It lay before us unyielding, impenetrable. Now the question is easier. We have four healthy children. Heidi is delightfully alternative and the others have benefited from her difference. We have learnt a lot about God and ourselves through the hard times we have been through.

But many others can't look back from a happy vantage point. They may still be right in the middle of the storm. There may be happy moments amidst the struggle, but there seems no prospect of coming out on the other side. Take the parents of a boy we met. He was very strong, yet unable to control his muscles. He could be very destructive, yet was unable to feed himself and could hardly communicate. A constant exhaustion, and no respite care available. Our inner reaction was to be thankful that our burden was so much lighter, which was no help to them.

Some may come through the trial, but for others there will never be a far side in this life. There are husbands and wives betrayed and abandoned by their partners. Parents whose children have died, or have rejected Jesus Christ. Others have deep secret pains; physical, mental or spiritual. Perhaps some people have read this book with incomprehension or anger: *'How can they be so ungrateful? They should feel what it's like to be unable to have any children'*. For these and many others there is no easy 'It was hard at the time, but now I understand'. When you can see no 'Because', how do you deal with the 'Why'?

Think of Job in the Bible. He often gets a bad press, which is pretty unfair considering what he went through. He seemed to have it made, didn't he? Ten children, seven thousand sheep, three thousand camels. I could go on. Then, in an instant, everything was gone. All his children killed in an accident. His livestock destroyed by fire or stolen by raiders. The man who had everything suddenly had nothing. Was God punishing him for some wicked deed? No, he feared God and hated evil. How does he react to this devastation of his life?

'The Lord gave and the Lord has taken away. May the name of the Lord be praised.'

You would think that if anyone had suffered enough, Job had. But then he became covered with painful sores from the soles of his feet to the top of his head. Does he give up on God now? No, his response is to say **'Shall we accept good from God, and not trouble?'**

Of course, Job struggled to cope with his miserable situation. He wished he had never been born. He couldn't understand why all this was happening to him and he poured out his frustration in torrents of questions to God. But he never let go of his faith in God. In the midst of such deep trouble, he still had the confidence to say '[God] **knows the way that I take. When he has tested me, I shall come forth as gold.'** Whether the gold would appear in this life or the next, Job didn't know. But he did know with unflinching certainty that God's plan would one day be seen to be right.

Healthy family, delightful Heidi, lessons learnt—yes, for us there is some truth in the answers to our 'Why' that I gave a little earlier. But ultimately they are deeply inadequate. God has given us many good things, but if he should choose to take them away again, our 'answers' are gone too. We still don't know what tomorrow holds.

'Steve! Come quickly! Heidi looks terrible.' I rushed upstairs. Heidi was lying in her bed, shivering uncontrollably. Her breathing was shallow, her pulse fast. She was purple all over, turning to blue at her fingers and toes. *Oh no, not this again.*

Soon I was on my way to hospital with her. Once more my mind was projecting a series of graphic images onto a screen in my head. Tubes, heart failure, consultant, pneumonia, machinery, leukaemia, operation, oxygen, breathing. A jumbled-up rapid-fire summary of those terrible times. *Please, not again.*

When we arrived at the hospital Heidi had brightened up a lot and all the symptoms were fading. And by the time the doctor saw her she was ready to play. I felt a bit of an idiot as she laughed and chatted with the doctor, clearly a picture of health.

I strapped her back into the car at midnight.

'We had great fun at the hostibal (sic) didn't we mummy', she grinned.

 Where was I? 'We still don't know what tomorrow holds'— or even today. This time we were so thankful that there was no problem. But the suddenness with which Heidi's health can deteriorate is unnerving. With Heidi the future is even more uncertain than for most of us, not only from a health perspective but in many other ways. One day she will no longer be a cute bundle of fun, and we can envisage many potential problems as she grows towards adulthood. Independence, accommodation, work, social life, relationships, prejudice. No doubt there are more unforeseen ones. Or maybe God will choose to take back to himself his creation whom he has loaned to us. Will we then start angrily asking 'Why' again?

As Job realised, in the end the only answer lies in the character of God. What we have experienced of this over these last few years has demonstrated what we knew to be true.

What do we deserve from God? He is the Holy Creator, ruler of the universe. We are his creations, his property, yet we are unable and sometimes unwilling to obey the blueprint he has given us to follow. We have done nothing to deserve his approval or merit his kindness. Yet he gave us a wonderful marriage and two healthy sons, amongst many other things we hardly noticed. He gave us these things not because we deserved them, but because he loves to give good things to his children. And how did we react to God's gift of a daughter? Because she wasn't the daughter we had envisaged, we threw the toys out of the pram. Yes, it was a shock, yes, it was a tough thing to deal with, yes, we fought our negative reactions. There may be nothing wrong in asking God why such a thing has happened to us. It is certainly better to express to him how we feel than to pretend we are not having such thoughts. But there is a world of difference between a perplexed yet submissive 'why' and a footstamping, rebellious 'why'. Too often ours tended towards the latter. We were kicking against God's will for us. Our expectation was of a 'perfect family'. We would have been horrified by the thought, but perhaps subconsciously we considered this was what we deserved. To react by saying 'It's not fair' implies 'We deserved something better'.

How did God respond to our ungracious attitude towards his gift? By continuing to be gracious. He gave us the support of loving friends and family. He provided excellent medical care. He preserved Heidi's life. He guided our decisions when we were at our wits' end. As we struggled to trust him he continued to demonstrate his total trustworthiness. Although we quickly reach the end of our meagre resources, we should have learnt by now that we can always depend on him.

So many times during those dark, mystifying months we felt totally out of control. We were, of course. Yet God was in complete control the whole time. From our perspective Heidi almost died any number of times. Her life was dangling by the merest of threads. But from God's viewpoint she was safer than the gold in Fort Knox. There was no chance of her dying, because his time had not come. That will continue to be true for the rest of her life and ours. Nothing will surprise him, and his plan is perfect.

'I didn't want the XL model, I wanted the Superlite Plus!' If this was your child's grumpy reaction to his birthday present, would you give him the Superlite Plus next year? Not I—but what did God give us? Another daughter. How gracious is that! Surely God has given us so much more than we deserve.

So then, if we know that God is wholly trustworthy, in total control and utterly good, we should be able to trust when we cannot see. As yet we can still only peer up at the underside of his beautiful tapestry. One day we will see, with a delighted intake of breath, God's whole perfect plan for us and Heidi. Until then, we must aim to stay focussed on that unchanging truth, through whatever difficulties may face us.

This chapter began with a fairy tale, because it may have appeared that our story finishes with a 'happily ever after'. It should now be clear that any notion of this is as illusory as any of the Grimms' finest. This book is not a fairy story, and this is not the end.

God has given us so much more than we deserve.